"THE DEFINITIVE GUIDE to shopping in Asia." – **Arthur Frommer**, The Arthur Frommer Almanac of Travel

"THE BEST travel book I've ever read." – Kathy Osiro, **TravelAge West**

"AN EXCELLENT, EXHAUSTIVE, AND FASCINATING look at shopping in the East . . . it's difficult to imagine a shopping tour without this pocket-size book in hand." – **Travel & Leisure**

"BOOKS IN THE SERIES help travelers recognize quality and gain insight to local customs." – **Travel-Holiday**

"THE BEST GUIDE I've seen on shopping in Asia. If you enjoy the sport, you'll find it hard to put down . . . They tell you not only the where and what of shopping but the important how, and all in enormous but easy-to-read detail." – **Seattle Post-Intelligencer**

"ONE OF THE BEST GUIDEBOOKS of the season—not just shopping strategies, but a Baedeker to getting around . . . definitely a quality work. Highly recommended." – **Arkansas Democrat**

"WILL WANT TO LOOK INTO . . . has shopping strategies and travel tips about making the most of a visit to those areas. The book covers Asia's shopping centers, department stores, emporiums, factory outlets, markets and hotel shopping arcades where visitors can find jewelry, leather goods, woodcarvings, textiles, antiques, cameras, and primitive artifacts." – **Chicago Tribune**

"FULL OF SUGGESTIONS. The art of bartering, including everyday shopping basics are clearly defined, along with places to hang your hat or lift a fork." – **The Washington Post**

"A WONDERFUL GUIDE . . . filled with essential tips as well as a lot of background information . . . a welcome addition on your trip." – **Travel Book Tips**

"WELL ORGANIZED AND COMPREHENSIVE BOOK. A useful companion for anyone planning a shopping spree in Asia." – **International Living**

"OFFERS SOME EXTREMELY VALUABLE INFORMATION and advice about what is all too often a spur-of-the-moment aspect of your overseas travel." – **Trip & Tour**

"A MORE UNUSUAL, PRACTICAL GUIDE than most and is no mere listing of convenience stores abroad . . . contains unusual tips on bargaining in Asia . . . country-specific tips are some of the most valuable chapters of the guidebook, setting it apart from others which may generalize upon Asia as a whole, or focus upon the well-known Hong Kong shopping pleasures." – **The Midwest Book Review**

"*I LOVED THE BOOK! Why didn't I have this book two months ago! . . . a valuable guide . . . very helpful for the first time traveler in Asia . . . worth packing in the suitcase for a return visit.*" – Editor, **Unique & Exotic Travel Reporter**

"*VERY USEFUL, PERFECTLY ORGANIZED. Finally a guide that combines Asian shopping opportunities with the tips and know-how to really get the best buys.*" – **National Motorist**

"*INFORMATION-PACKED PAGES point out where the best shops are located, how to save time when shopping, and where and when to deal . . . You'll be a smarter travel shopper if you follow the advice of this new book.*" – **AAA World**

"*DETAILED, AND RELEVANT, EVEN ABSORBING in places . . . The authors know their subject thoroughly, and the reader can benefit greatly from their advice and tips. They go a long way to removing any mystery or uneasiness about shopping in Asia by the neophyte.*" – **The Small Press Book Review**

WHAT SEASONED TRAVELERS SAY

"*IMMENSELY USEFUL . . . thanks for sharing the fruits of your incredibly thorough research. You saved me hours of time and put me in touch with the best.*" – **C.N.**, DeKalb, Illinois

"*FABULOUS! I've just returned from my third shopping trip to Southeast Asia in three years. This book, which is now wrinkled, torn, and looking much abused, has been my bible for the past three years. All your suggestions (pre-trip) and information was so great. When I get ready to go again, my 'bible,' even though tattered and torn, will accompany me again! Thanks again for all your wonderful knowledge, and for sharing it!*" – **D.P.**, Havertown, Pennsylvania

"*I LOVE IT. I've read a lot of travel books, and of all the books of this nature, this is the best I've ever read. Especially for first timers, the how-to information is invaluable.*" – **A.K.**, Portland, Oregon

"*THE BEST TRAVEL BOOK I'VE EVER READ. Believe me, I know my travel books!*" – **S.T.**, Washington, DC

"*MANY MANY THANKS for your wonderful, useful travel guide! You have done a tremendous job. It is so complete and precise and full of neat info.*" – **K.H.**, Seattle, Washington

"*FABULOUS BOOK! I just came back from Hong Kong, Thailand, and Singapore and found your book invaluable. Every place you recommended I found wonderful quality shopping. Send me another copy for my friend in Singapore who was fascinated with it.*" – **M.G.**, Escondido, California

"*THIS IS MY FIRST FAN LETTER . . . you made our trip more special than I can ever say.*" – **N.H.**, New York, New York

THE TREASURES AND PLEASURES OF RIO AND SÃO PAULO

By Drs. Ron and Caryl Krannich

TRAVEL AND INTERNATIONAL BOOKS

International Jobs Directory
Jobs For People Who Love to Travel
Mayors and Managers in Thailand
Politics of Family Planning Policy in Thailand
Shopping and Traveling in Exotic Asia
Shopping in Exotic Places
Shopping the Exotic South Pacific
Travel Planning on the Internet
Treasures and Pleasures of Australia
Treasures and Pleasures of China
Treasures and Pleasures of Egypt
Treasures and Pleasures of Hong Kong
Treasures and Pleasures of India
Treasures and Pleasures of Indonesia
Treasures and Pleasures of Israel and Jordan
Treasures and Pleasures of Italy
Treasures and Pleasures of Morocco
Treasures and Pleasures of Paris and the French Riviera
Treasures and Pleasures of the Philippines
Treasures and Pleasures of Rio and São Paulo
Treasures and Pleasures of Singapore and Bali
Treasures and Pleasures of Singapore and Malaysia
Treasures and Pleasures of Thailand
Treasures and Pleasures of Vietnam

BUSINESS AND CAREER BOOKS AND SOFTWARE

101 Dynamite Answers to Interview Questions
101 Secrets of Highly Effective Speakers
201 Dynamite Job Search Letters
America's Top Internet Sites
Best Jobs For the 21st Century
Change Your Job, Change Your Life
The Complete Guide to International Jobs and Careers
The Complete Guide to Public Employment
The Directory of Federal Jobs and Employers
Discover the Best Jobs For You!
Dynamite Cover Letters
Dynamite Networking For Dynamite Jobs
Dynamite Resumes
Dynamite Salary Negotiations
Dynamite Tele-Search
The Educator's Guide to Alternative Jobs and Careers
Find a Federal Job Fast!
From Air Force Blue to Corporate Gray
From Army Green to Corporate Gray
From Navy Blue to Corporate Gray
Get a Raise in 7 Days
High Impact Resumes and Letters
Interview For Success
Job-Power Source CD-ROM
Jobs and Careers With Nonprofit Organizations
Military Resumes and Cover Letters
Moving Out of Education
Moving Out of Government
Re-Careering in Turbulent Times
Resumes & Job Search Letters For Transitioning Military Personnel
Savvy Interviewing
Savvy Networker
Savvy Resume Writer
Ultimate Job Source CD-ROM

IMPACT GUIDES

THE TREASURES
AND PLEASURES OF

Rio & São Paulo

BEST OF THE BEST IN
TRAVEL AND SHOPPING

RON AND CARYL KRANNICH, PH.DS

IMPACT PUBLICATIONS
MANASSAS PARK, VA

www.iShopAroundTheWorld.com

THE TREASURES AND PLEASURES OF RIO AND SÃO PAULO

Cover Photo Credits: Cover photos are courtesy of RIOTUR, the City of Rio de Janeiro Tourism Authority. For information on their services and the city of Rio, see page 113 as well as visit RIOTUR's websites: *www.rio.rj.gov.br/riotur* and *www.destinationrio.com*.

Library of Congress Cataloguing-in-Publication Data

Krannich, Ronald L.
    The treasures and pleasures of Rio and São Paulo: best of
      the best in travel and shopping / Ron and Caryl Krannich
        p. cm. – (Impact guides)
    Includes bibliographical references and index.
    ISBN 1-57023-152-4
    1. Shopping – Brazil – Rio de Janeiro – Guidebooks.
    2. Shopping – Brazil – São Paulo – Guidebooks.
    I. Krannich, Caryl Rae. II. Title. III. Series.

    TX337.B62 K73 2001
    380.1'45'0002581 – dc21   2001024049

Publisher: For information on Impact Publications, including current and forthcoming publications, authors, press kits, websites online bookstores, and submission requirements, visit Impact's main website: *www.impactpublications.com*. For addition information on this and other books in the series, see these related websites: *www.ishoparoundtheworld.com* and *www.contentfortravel.com*

Publicity/Rights: For information on publicity, author interviews, and subsidiary rights, contact the Media Relations Department: Tel. 703-361-7300, Fax 703-361-7300, or email: *rio@impactpub lications.com*.

Sales/Distribution: All bookstore sales are handled through Impact's trade distributor: National Book Network, 15200 NBN Way, Blue Ridge Summit, PA 17214, Tel. 1-800-462-6420. All other sales and distribution inquiries should be directed to the publisher: Sales Department, IMPACT PUBLICATIONS, 9104 Manassas Drive, Suite N, Manassas Park, VA 20111-5211, Tel. 703-361-7300, Fax 703-335-9486, or email: *sales@impactpublica tions.com*.

Contents

Preface

WELCOME TO ANOTHER IMPACT GUIDE that explores the many unique treasures and pleasures of shopping and traveling in two of Brazil's most fascinating cities – Rio and São Paulo. Join us as we explore these cities's many treasures and pleasures, from great shops and top restaurants to fine hotels, sightseeing, and entertainment. We'll put you in touch with the best of the best these places have to offer visitors. We'll take you to popular tourist destinations, but we won't linger long since *lifestyle shopping* is our travel passion – combining great shopping with terrific dining. If you follow us to the end, you'll discover a whole new dimension to both Brazil and travel. Indeed, as the following pages unfold, you'll learn there is a lot more to Brazil, and travel in general, than taking tours, visiting popular sites, and acquiring an unwelcome weight gain attendant with new on-the-road dining habits.

Exciting Rio and São Paulo offer wonderful travel experiences for those who know what to look for, where to go, and how to properly travel and shop its major destinations. While these cities are popular destinations for visiting beaches, rainforests, colonial buildings, churches, festivals, and obscure historical sites that often characterize Brazil's travel image, for us both Rio and São Paulo also are important shopping destinations that yield unique jewelry, art, antiques, and crafts as well as excellent restaurants, hotels, entertainment, and outdoor sports. Their people, products, sights, and sounds have truly enriched our lives.

If you are familiar with our other Impact Guides, you know this will not be another standard travel guide to history, culture, and sightseeing in Brazil. Our approach to travel is very different. We operate from a particular perspective, and we frequently show our attitude rather than just present you with the sterile "travel facts." While we seek good travel value, we're not budget travelers who are interested in taking you along the low road to Rio and São Paulo. We've been there, done that at one stage in our lives. If that's the way you want to go, you'll find lots of guidebooks on budget travel to Brazil as well as a whole travel industry geared toward servicing budget travelers and backpackers with everything from hostels to Internet cafés. At the same time, we're not obsessed with local history, culture, and sightseeing. We get just enough history and sightseeing to make our travels interesting rather than obsessive. Accordingly, we include very little on history and sightseeing, because they are not our main focus; we also assume you have that information covered from other resources. When we discuss history and sightseeing, we do so in abbreviated form, highlighting what we consider to be the essentials. As you'll quickly discover, we're very focused – we're in search of quality shopping and travel. Rather than spend eight hours a day sightseeing, we may only devote two hours to sightseeing and another six hours learning about the local shopping scene. As such, we're very people- and product-oriented when we travel. Through shopping, we meet many interesting and talented people and learn a great deal about their country.

What we really enjoy doing, and think we do it well, is shop. For us, shopping makes for great travel adventure. Indeed, we're street people who love "the chase" and the serendipity that comes with our style of travel. We especially enjoy discovering quality products; meeting local artists and craftspeople; unraveling new travel and shopping rules; making new friendships with local business people; staying in fine places; and

❏ Our approach to travel is very different from most guidebooks.

❏ We're not obsessed with local history, culture, and sightseeing. We get just enough history and sightseeing to make our travels interesting rather than obsessive.

❏ Through shopping, we meet many interesting and talented people and learn a great deal about their country.

❏ We're street people who love "the chase" and the serendipity that comes with our style of travel.

dining in the best restaurants where we often meet the talented chefs and visit their fascinating kitchens. In the cases of Rio and São Paulo, we seek the best quality jewelry, arts, antiques, crafts, and apparel as well as discover the best artists and craftspeople. In so doing, we learn a great deal about present Brazil and its talented population.

The chapters that follow represent a particular perspective. We purposefully decided to write more than just another travel guide with a few pages on shopping. While some travel guides include a brief and usually dated section on the "whats" and "wheres" of shopping, we saw a need to also explain the "how-tos" of shopping in Rio and São Paulo. Such a book would both educate and guide you through Brazil's shopping maze – from finding great gems and jewelry and navigating numerous weekend markets to getting the best deals and arranging for the shipping of large items – as well as put you in contact with the best of the best in restaurants, accommodations, and sightseeing. It would be a combination travel-shopping guide designed for people in search of quality travel experiences.

The perspective we develop throughout this book is based on our belief that traveling should be more than just another adventure in eating, sleeping, sightseeing, and taking pictures of unfamiliar places. Whenever possible, we attempt to bring to life the fact that Brazil has real people and interesting products that you, the visitor, will find exciting. This is a country of very talented artists, craftspeople, traders, and entrepreneurs. When you leave Brazil, you will take with you not only some unique experiences and memories but also quality products that you will certainly appreciate for years to come.

We have not hesitated to make qualitative judgments about the best of the best in Rio and São Paulo. If we just presented you with travel and shopping information, we would do you a disservice by not sharing our discoveries, both good and bad. While we know that our judgments may not be valid for everyone, we offer them as **reference points** from which you can make your own decisions. Our major emphasis is on quality shopping, dining, accommodations, sightseeing, and entertainment, and in that order. We look for shops which offer excellent quality and styles. If you share our concern for quality shopping, as well as fine restaurants and hotels, you will find many of our recommendations useful to planning and implementing your Brazilian adventure. Best of all, you'll engage in what has become a favorite pastime for many of today's discerning travelers – lifestyle shopping!

Throughout this book we have included "tried and tested" shopping information. We make judgments based upon our experience – not on judgments or sales pitches from others. Our research method was quite simple: we did a great deal of shopping and we looked for quality products. We acquired some fabulous items, and gained valuable knowledge in the process. However, we could not make purchases in every shop nor do we have any guarantee that your experiences will be the same as ours. Shops close, ownership or management changes, and the shop you visit may not be the same as the one we shopped. So use this information as a starting point, but ask questions and make your own judgments before you buy.

Whatever you do, enjoy Rio and São Paulo. While you need not *"shop 'til you drop,"* at least shop these places well and with the confidence that you are getting good quality and value. Don't just limit yourself to small items that will fit into your suitcase or pass up something you love because of shipping concerns. Consider acquiring larger items that can be safely and conveniently shipped back home. Indeed, shipping is something that needs to be *arranged* rather than lamented or avoided.

We wish to thank the many people who contributed to this book. They include many shop owners and personnel who took time to educate us on their products and the local shopping, dining, and travel scenes. They also include many hotel personnel, from concierges to front desk personnel at the Copacabana Palace Hotel in Rio and the L'Hotel in São Paulo, who went several extra steps to ensure that we were well informed about the best of the best in their cities. These knowledgeable individuals also exemplify some of the best service you will find anywhere in the hospitality industry – a genuine and enthusiastic service ethic and a contagious positive attitude toward their cities. We truly appreciated their assistance and highly recommend their extraordinary properties to fellow travelers. We also wish to thank Mardie Younglof who did the final editing and RIOTUR for supplying cover photos.

We wish you well as you prepare for Brazil's many treasures and pleasures. The book is designed to be used in the streets of these two cities. If you **plan** your journey according to the first four chapters and **navigate** our two major destinations based on the next two chapters, you should have an absolutely marvelous time. You'll discover some exciting places, acquire some choice items, and return home with many fond memories of a terrific adventure. If you put this book to use, it will indeed become your best friend – and passport – to the many unique treasures and pleasures of Rio and São Paulo. Enjoy!

Ron and Caryl Krannich
krannich@impactpublications.com

Liabilities and Warranties

Wᴴᴵᴸᴇ ᴛʜᴇ ᴀᴜᴛʜᴏʀs ʜᴀᴠᴇ ᴀᴛᴛᴇᴍᴘᴛᴇᴅ
to provide accurate information, please remember that names, addresses, phone and fax numbers, email addresses, and website URLs do change and shops, restaurants, and hotels do move, go out of business, or change ownership and management. Such changes are a constant fact of life in ever-changing Rio and São Paulo. We regret any inconvenience such changes may cause to your travel and shopping plans.

Inclusion of shops, restaurants, hotels, and other hospitality providers in this book in no way implies guarantees nor endorsements by either the authors or publisher. The information and recommendations appearing in this book are provided solely for your reference. The honesty and reliability of shops can best be ensured by **you** – always ask the right questions, request proper receipts and documents, and observe the many shopping rules outlined in Chapter 3, especially pages 39-50.

The Treasures and Pleasures of Rio and São Paulo provides numerous tips on how you can best experience a trouble-free adventure. As in any unfamiliar place or situation, and regardless of how trusting strangers may appear, the watch-words are always the same – *"watch your wallet!"* If it seems too good to be true, it probably is. Any *"unbelievable deals"* should be treated as such. In Brazil, as elsewhere in the world, there simply is no such thing as a free lunch. Everything has a cost. Just make sure you don't pay dearly by making unnecessary shopping mistakes!

The Treasures and Pleasures of Rio and São Paulo

Welcome to Rio and São Paulo

WELCOME TO BRAZIL'S, AND SOUTH AMERica's, two greatest cities. For travelers who love big, vibrant, and romantic cities offering great shopping, dining, accommodations, sightseeing, entertainment, and culture, it doesn't get much better than seductive Rio and elegant São Paulo. With a combined population of 30 million, these two cities represent 17 percent of the country's total population of 172 million. While they may not represent the "real" Brazil, they at least represent two very special parts of Brazil that you should not miss as you visit this vast and diverse country. Even unto themselves, they represent different Brazilian urban styles – Rio the beautiful, vibrant, and beached party town and São Paulo the monstrous business and industrial center. Visiting these two cities will immerse you in the many wonderful treasures and pleasures of Brazil. Whatever you do, don't miss these two cities on your next trip to Brazil. They will not disappoint you.

GETTING TO KNOW YOU

We love traveling to many of the world's great cities, be it London, Paris, Rome, Cairo, Bombay, Bangkok, Singapore,

Hong Kong, Shanghai, Tokyo, Sydney, Toronto, New York, or Mexico City. The people, places, architecture, traffic, sites, shops, culture, entertainment, restaurants, hotels, and even the frequent living chaos all add up to many exciting adventures. It's in these cities, with their rich tapestries of sights, sounds, and consumables, where we tend to experience many magical moments. And it's these cities that make travel a great adventure in quality shopping, sightseeing, dining, and accommodations. The cities often represent the best of the best a country has to offer, even though they simultaneously showcase many of the worst aspects of their societies, such as crime, poverty, and social dislocation.

❑ With a combined population of 30 million, Rio and São Paulo represent 17 percent of Brazil's total population.

❑ We love traveling to many of the world's great cities. It's these cities that often represent the best of the best a country has to offer.

❑ Rio is one of the world's great visual cities with spectacular hillside, beach, and harbor views reminiscent of Hong Kong, Monaco, and Sydney.

❑ São Paulo is a relatively sophisticated city of business and culture where you will find many of Brazil's best shops, restaurants, hotels, and cultural and entertainment centers.

Getting to know our cities takes some special effort beyond joining guided tours or following guidebooks, maps, and a compass. Somewhat intimidating for first-time visitors, our cities require a sense of adventure as one navigates through miles of unfamiliar streets in search of many unique treasures and pleasures that only these cities possess. If you are like us, you'll find your urban adventure to be very rewarding from the moment you arrive until the time you depart.

THE TALES OF TWO CITIES

Traveling to Brazil inevitably puts you in touch with either Rio or São Paulo, but hopefully both cities. After all, there's a very good chance your international transportation will land and you'll disembark in one of these cities. If you visit sensuous Rio, you'll be visiting one of the world's great visual cities with spectacular hillside, beach, and harbor views reminiscent of Hong Kong, Monaco, and Sydney. Boasting nearly 10 million people, Rio is a vibrant city of great character, style, and culture, with its beautiful beaches, granite outcrops, efficient subway system and, as they say in Rio, "beautiful people" or *cariocas* who populate the throbbing beaches, bars, restaurants, and cafes along the beachfront streets that ring the city's major beach, hotel, dining, entertainment, and shopping districts.

This is the city of the famous Corcovado, the 710-meter peak with the huge statute of Christ the Redeemer with arms outstretched and overlooking the city, and the popular hill of Pão de Açúcar, or Sugar Loaf; both places compete in offering the most spectacular views of the city and surrounding area of beaches, ocean, and mountains. Rio also is the city of the annual glitzy, gay, and often overly exuberant Carnival.

Any way you look at it, much of Rio is all about enjoying the good life of beaches, bodies, booze, music, dance, shopping, and dining. With lots of great things to see and do, Rio is a fun city for most visitors as well as many residents who can afford its many pleasures. Known as Latin America's playground, Rio is an especially great city to go treasure hunting for gems, jewelry, antiques, and handicrafts. While Rio also has its dark sides, from the poverty of its hillside shantytowns (*favalas*) to crime and violence, hopefully during your short stay you will concentrate on Rio's many treasures and pleasures that especially appeal to the interests and tastes of international visitors.

São Paulo, on the other hand, is twice as large as Rio with a population of nearly 20 million. It can be an intimidating city because of its sheer size. However, it's a much smaller city when it comes to shopping, because the major shopping areas are very concentrated in one area. While São Paulo is not as visually spectacular nor as much outdoor fun as Rio – because it lacks a playful beach and Carnival culture – São Paulo is a relatively sophisticated city of business and culture with its own unique beauty and fun. A major industrial and financial center, São Paulo is Latin America's economic powerhouse. Its tall buildings, wide boulevards, bustling side streets, museums, and cultural centers give this city a truly international character. A vibrant and cosmopolitan city noted for its large number of Italian and Japanese immigrants, with their own ethnic neighborhoods, São Paulo is where you will find many of Brazil's best shops, restaurants, hotels, and cultural and entertainment centers. Its weekend markets and shopping delights, including shopping in the nearby towns of Itu and Embu, are some of the best in Brazil. While São Paulo also has its downsides, from traffic and pollution to crime and violence, nonetheless, it's a great city well worth a few days of your attention, especially when it comes to fine shopping and dining.

A UNIQUE PERSPECTIVE

The pages that follow are not your typical nor redundant treatment of travel to Rio and São Paulo. Indeed, there are numerous guidebooks available on Brazil and these two cities that basically focus on variations of the same themes – history, sightseeing, accommodations, restaurants, and entertainment. Many go into extreme detail on the history and culture of each city, with special emphasis on Rio's beach and Carnival culture. Some guidebooks even recommend avoiding these two cities, because they don't represent the "real" Brazil; instead, they take you into secondary cities or up the Amazon River to meet another group of "beautiful people." Numerous budget guides touting the oft repeated *"I'm a traveler, not a tourist"* philosophy outline how to experience inexpensive Brazil on your own by providing a generous offering of cheap restaurants, hotels, and transportation. If this is your primary interest and style of travel, you'll find many useful guidebooks that offer this approach to Rio, São Paulo, and greater Brazil. However, if this is not your primary travel passion (you get anxious after hours in a museum or at a historic site) and you prefer a different level (class) of travel experience (you're not opposed to five-star hotels and restaurants as well as prefer a car and driver to a crowded bus), you may find such guidebooks less than welcome additions to your luggage.

❑ Our primary focus is on quality travel and shopping in Rio and São Paulo.

❑ We learned long ago that one of the best ways to meet the local people and experience another culture is to go shopping.

❑ One of our missions is to help promote and support the continuing development of local arts and crafts through shopping.

❑ We've attempted to identify the best quality shopping in Rio and São Paulo, with a decided emphasis on shopping for unique and quality items that will retain their value in the long run and can be appreciated for years to come.

❑ We also tend to be lifestyle shoppers – enjoy combining great restaurants and sightseeing with our many shopping sojourns.

Like other volumes in the Impact Guides series and the content found on our companion *iShopAroundThe World.com* website, this book focuses on quality travel and shopping in Rio and São Paulo. Yes, shopping. We learned long ago that one of the most enjoyable aspects of travel, and one of the best ways to meet the local people and experience another culture, is to shop its many department stores, shops, markets, factories, and galleries. In so doing, we explore the fascinating worlds of artisans, craftspeople, and shopkeepers where we discover quality products, outstanding buys, and talented, interesting, and friendly people. In addition, one of our missions is to help promote and support the continuing development of local arts and crafts. For us, travel-shopping makes for a great and mutually rewarding adventure.

A TRAVEL-SHOPPING EMPHASIS

Much of *The Treasures and Pleasures of Rio and São Paulo* is designed to provide you with the necessary **knowledge and skills** to become an effective travel-shopper. We especially designed the book with two major considerations in mind:

- Focus on quality shopping
- Emphasis on finding unique items

Throughout this book we attempt to identify the **best quality shopping** in Rio and São Paulo. This does not mean we have discovered the cheapest shopping nor best bargains, although we have attempted to do so when opportunities for comparative shopping arose within and between communities. Our focus is primarily on shopping for **unique and quality items** that will retain their value in the long run and can be appreciated for years to come. This means many of our recommended shops may initially appear expensive. But they offer top value that you will not find in many other shops. For example, when we discover unique jewelers in Rio, we acknowledge the fact that their work is expensive, but it is very beautiful and unique, so much so that you quickly forget their prices after you acquire and continue to admire their outstanding work. At the same time, we identify what we consider to be the best buys for various items, especially jewelry, antiques, furniture, and handicrafts. The same is true in the case of arts and antiques in São Paulo.

APPROACHING THE SUBJECT

The chapters that follow take you on a whirlwind travel adventure of Rio and São Paulo with a decided emphasis on quality shopping, dining, and sightseeing. We literally put a shopping face on Rio and São Paulo, one that we believe you will thoroughly enjoy as you explore Rio and São Paulo's many other pleasures. While we enjoy shopping when traveling abroad, we're not overly obsessive about it. Indeed, we tend to be lifestyle shoppers – enjoy combining great restaurants and sightseeing with our many shopping sojourns. Nonetheless, shopping takes center stage in our travel adventures.

Our **choice of cities** – Rio and São Paulo – should come as no surprise given the fact that most quality shopping and travel amenities tend to gravitate to Brazil's two major cities. These are the places many tourists and business people travel to and thus where you will find the best of the best Brazil has to offer travelers and shoppers.

We've given a great deal of attention to constructing a complete **user-friendly book** that focuses on the shopping process, offers extensive details on the "how," "what," and "where" of shopping, and includes a sufficient level of redundancy to be informative, useful, and usable. The chapters, for example, are organized like one would organize and implement a travel-shopping adventure. Each chapter incorporates sufficient details, including names and addresses, to get you started in some of the best shopping areas and shops in each city.

Indexes and table of contents are especially important to us and others who believe a travel book is first and foremost a guide to unfamiliar places. Therefore, our index includes both subjects and shops, with shops printed in bold for ease of reference; the table of contents is elaborated in detail so it, too, can be used as another handy reference index for subjects and products. If, for example, you are interested in "what to buy" or "where to shop" in Rio, the best reference will be the table of contents. If you are interested in markets in Rio, look under "markets" in the index. And if you are interested in learning where you can find good quality art in São Paulo, then look under "art" in the index section for São Paulo. By using the table of contents and index together, you can access most any information from this book.

The remainder of this book is divided into two parts and five additional chapters which look at both the process and content of traveling and shopping in Rio and São Paulo. Part I – **"Smart Traveling and Shopping"** – assists you in preparing for your Brazilian adventure by focusing on the how-to of traveling and shopping. Chapter 2, **"Know Before You Go,"** takes you through the basics of getting to and enjoying your stay throughout Brazil. It includes advice on when to go, what to pack, required documents, currency, business hours, international and domestic transportation, tipping, tourist offices, useful websites, and local customs. Chapter 3, **"Shopping Treasures and Rules For Success,"** examines Rio's and São Paulo's major shopping strengths, from jewelry and antiques to clothes and handicrafts. It also includes lots of advice on comparative shopping, shopping tips, and shipping strategies for shopping in Rio and São Paulo. Chapter 4, **"Buying Gems and Jewelry,"** is presented as a primer for purchasing what often becomes two of the most difficult big ticket items for travelers – gems and jewelry. As you'll quickly discover in Rio and São Paulo, gemstones and jewelry are everywhere. Like other visitors to Brazil, you'll be tempted to make such purchases. In Chapter 4, we provide some important advice on what to look for when making what often becomes an impulsive or spontaneous purchase under pressure.

The two chapters in Part II—"**Great Destinations**"— examine the how, what, and where of traveling and shopping in and around both Rio and São Paulo. Here we identify major shopping strengths of each place; detail the best of the best of shopping; and share information on some of the best hotels, restaurants, and sightseeing for each city and surrounding area.

OUR RECOMMENDATIONS

We hesitate to recommend specific shops, restaurants, hotels, and sites since we know the pitfalls of doing so. Shops that offered excellent products and service during one of our visits, for example, may change ownership, personnel, and policies from one year to another, or they may suddenly move to another location or go out of business. In addition, our shopping preferences may not be the same as your preferences. The same is true for restaurants, hotels, and sites: they do change.

Since we put shopping up front in our travels to Rio and São Paulo, our major concern is to outline your shopping options, show you where to locate the best shopping areas, and share some useful shopping strategies that you can use anywhere in these cities, regardless of particular shops or markets we or others may recommend. Armed with this knowledge and some basic shopping skills, you will be better prepared to locate your own shops and determine which ones offer the best products and service in relation to your own shopping and travel goals.

However, we also recognize the "need to know" when shopping in unfamiliar places. Therefore, throughout this book we list the names and locations of various shops we have found to offer good quality products. In some cases we have purchased items in these shops and can also recommend them for service and reliability. But in most cases we surveyed shops to determine the quality of products offered without making purchases. To buy in every shop would be beyond our budget, as well as our home storage capabilities! Whatever you do, treat our names and addresses as **orientation points** from which to identify your own products and shops. If you rely solely on our listings, you will miss out on one of the great adventures of shopping in Rio and São Paulo – discovering your own special shops that offer unique items and exceptional value and service.

The same holds true for our recommendations on hotels,

restaurants, sightseeing, and entertainment. We sought out the best of the best in these major "travel pleasure" areas. You should find most of our recommendations useful in organizing your own special Rio and São Paulo adventure.

EXPECT A REWARDING ADVENTURE

Whatever you do, enjoy your adventure to Rio and São Paulo as you open yourself to a whole new world of travel-shopping. We're confident you'll discover some very special treasures and pleasures that will also make Brazil one of your favorite destinations.

So arrange your flights and accommodations, pack your credit cards and traveler's checks, and head for two of South America's most delightful destinations. One to two weeks later you should return home with much more than a set of photos and travel brochures. You will have some wonderful purchases and travel tales that can be enjoyed and relived for a lifetime.

Shopping and traveling in Rio and São Paulo only takes time, money, and a sense of adventure. Take the time, be willing to part with some of your money, and open yourself to a whole new world of travel. If you are like us, the treasures and pleasures outlined in this book will introduce you to an exciting world of quality products, friendly people, and interesting places that you might have otherwise missed had you just passed through Rio and São Paulo to eat, sleep, see sites, relax on the beach, and take pictures. When you travel our Rio and São Paulo, you're much more than a typical tourist or traveler – whether driven by a tour group or a self-directed travel guidebook – who only sees the popular travel highlights of these places. With us, you are a special kind of international visitor or guest – a travel-shopper – who discovers quality and learns about these places through the people and products that continue to define their culture. Best of all, you help support the local economies and promote talented individuals by purchasing quality arts, crafts, and other products that reflect the uniqueness of Brazil.

PART I

Smart Traveling
and Shopping

Know Before You Go

W HILE RIO AND SÃO PAULO ARE RELATIVE-
ly easy destinations to get to and around in,
there are certain things you should know about
them before you go. What, for example, is the
best time of the year to visit these places? How
should you pack? Can you expect to encounter language
problems? Should you take a group tour or travel independ-
ently? What kind of documents do you need? As a shopper,
what can you legally export or import? Are Brazilian gems and
jewelry dutiable? Are there any particular websites that can help
you plan your trip to Rio and São Paulo?

Answers to these and many other basic travel questions can
help you better prepare for your Brazilian travel-shopping
adventure. They are addressed in this pre-trip planning chapter.

LOCATION AND GEOGRAPHY

Located in the prosperous Southeast region of Brazil – the
country's industrial, mineral, agricultural, and tourism center
with 45 percent of the population – Rio and São Paulo are the
country's two largest cities and ports. They also boast the best
tourist and business infrastructures in the country, with lots of

good hotels, restaurants, shops, entertainment, and sightseeing opportunities. Beautiful beaches, tropical rainforests, and lovely mountains make Rio one of the world's most visually spectacular cities. A festive and laid-back city, Rio especially attracts travelers seeking a fun and relaxing holiday that takes advantage of the city's unique geographic location.

Located only a short 45-minute flight southwest of Rio, São Paulo is Brazil's New York. Sprawling over a flat plain, this huge inland industrial and financial city is within only a half hour of several beautiful beaches and colonial towns that provide escape from the hectic urban lifestyle. Towering office buildings, wonderful restaurants, great shops, and interesting markets make São Paulo a very attractive destination for travelers in search of Brazil's many treasures and pleasures that go beyond the well-worn tourist paths. Unlike Rio, São Paulo is not a city of great physical beauty. It has its attractive parks and architecture, but it's a relatively flat, crowded, and expansive megalopolis.

❑ Rio and São Paulo are the country's two largest cities and ports.

❑ Rio especially attracts travelers seeking a fun and relaxing holiday.

❑ São Paulo is Brazil's New York – towering buildings, wonderful restaurants, great shops, and interesting markets make it a very attractive destination.

❑ The best times to visit these two cities are in the spring and fall – April to June and August to October.

CLIMATE AND WHEN TO GO

Since Rio and São Paulo are in the southern hemisphere, their seasons are just the opposite of the northern hemisphere. Winter runs from June to September; the summer months are from December to March; fall occurs from April to May; and spring is from October to November. Since both cities are tropical, with Rio boasting one of the world's largest urban rainforests, the weather in both cities is relatively pleasant all year long, with average daily temperatures fluctuating from mid 60°F to mid 80°F. However, summers can be very hot and humid with beaches adding welcome relief from the steamy cities. Since São Paulo is located inland and in the highlands, its temperate is less tropical and fluctuates more than Rio's.

In terms of weather, the best times to visit these two cities are in the spring and fall, especially the months of April to June and August to October. The off-season period, when travel bargains are more prevalent, are the months of May, June, August, and September. July is the traditional school holiday period, and mid-December through February are high season months with crowded beaches, hotels, restaurants, and sightseeing attractions. However, you will often find very good travel bargains to Rio even during these high season months, with the four-day Carnival extravaganza excepted. Carnival, which occurs in either February or March of each year, is especially festive and crowded in Rio. Plan to book your flights and accommodations well in advance for this unique event.

WHAT TO PACK AND WEAR

Given Rio's and São Paulo's tropical climate and informal lifestyle, plan to pack as if you were visiting New Orleans or Atlanta – lightweight cotton clothing is especially important for summer. Since the weather can be tricky in São Paulo, you want to be prepared for some cooler temperatures. Rio is the more casual city with great deference given to outdoor beachfront activities. Pack for this city as you would most resorts that have few dress restrictions. Even the best restaurants in Rio do not require formal attire.

On the other hand, São Paulo is more formal and fashionable, tending toward smart casual for attire, than Rio. Since this is a major business city, its dress requirements are more in line with New York City than Miami. Few dining and entertainment establishments require formal attire, but many expect patrons to dress appropriately which is usually smart casual. If you are visiting São Paulo on important business, expect to wear a coat and tie and/or suit to your business meetings. The watchwords for dress in São Paulo are business, smart casual, and casual. The beaches are at least a half hour from the city where dress becomes more resort-oriented and thus more like Rio.

Since both cities are walking cities for shoppers and sightseers and Rio has its attractive beaches, you are well advised to take the following items:

Essentials:

- comfortable walking shoes
- sunglasses

Optional:

- umbrella
- camera
- compass

- swim gear
- hat or cap

Pack your camera and plenty of film for Rio. This city is a photographer's delight. In many elevated parts of the city, everywhere you turn seems to have spectacular views of the ocean, beaches, mountains, tropical rainforest, landmarks, and buildings perched on hillsides. You'll probably want to shoot this city many times. A compass comes in especially handy since you may frequently become disoriented by streets, subways, and maps which often lack important details. Our compass keeps us on track and helps us get to our destinations.

REQUIRED DOCUMENTS

Getting into Brazil is both convenient and inconvenient, depending on your nationality. Nationals of some countries only need a valid passport. Nationals of other countries, such as the U.S. and Canada, encounter archaic visa requirements. In the case of U.S. citizens, part of the blame for this situation is due to the U.S. State Department. Brazil believes in reciprocity. Indeed, it likes to "get even" for U.S. visa restrictions imposed on Brazilian citizens wishing to visit the U.S. who have to go through similar bureaucratic hurtles.

Consequently, all U.S. citizens entering Brazil need a valid passport (good for at least six months after entering Brazil) and a visa which is good for five years. Visas can be obtained through a Brazilian Embassy or consulate. With your application, you'll need to provide a passport-size photo (2" x 2"), confirmation of round-trip transportation to Brazil (photo copy of the actual ticket or a letter from a travel agent with a confirmation of the ticket), and $45 for processing the visa (cash, money order, certified check, or company check made payable to the Brazilian Embassy). As we go to press, the embassy in Washington, DC limits its jurisdiction by only accepting visa applications submitted by mail from residents of the District of Columbia, Kentucky, Ohio, Maryland, Virginia, and West Virginia and will only return documents by the U.S. Postal Service if you submit a self-addressed stamped envelope with your application; they will not use courier services or even FedEx or UPS. Residents of other states can apply in person or they must use Brazilian consulates which are found in Atlanta, Boston, Chicago, Houston, Los Angeles, Miami, New York, San Francisco, and San Juan. Office hours are from 8am to 5pm, Monday through Friday; you can only apply in person from

8am to 1pm. For more information, including a downloadable visa application form, visit the embassy's website and click onto "Consular Services":

www.brasilemb.org

The visa application form can be found by clicking on the "Application Form" button which appears in the upper right hand corner of the "Consular Services" page. The site also includes information on a variety of other types of visas. As you'll quickly discover, this is not a simple bureaucracy trying to encourage you to visit their country.

Citizens from other countries have similar visa requirements, but the fees and requirements may differ depending on reciprocal relationships with each country. Australians, for example, need a visa but

❑ Pack for Rio and São Paulo as if you were visiting New Orleans or Atlanta.

❑ Few dining and entertainment establishments require formal attire.

❑ Pack your camera and plenty of film for Rio – it's a photographer's delight.

❑ Brazil believes in reciprocity when it comes to required documents and fees – they make the visa application process equally inconvenient for North Americans.

❑ The peoples of Rio and São Paulo represent a fascinating mixture of different races and cultures.

there is no fee for it. Citizens from the United Kingdom, France, and 45 other countries only need a valid passport – no visa requirement. Canadian citizens need a visa which costs $40.

THE PEOPLES

The peoples of Rio and São Paulo represent a fascinating mixture of different races and cultures. They also exude a certain energetic and optimistic attitude toward life. A great melting pot of colonial Portuguese, indigenous Indian, imported African, and immigrant Japanese, Italians, Germans, Russians, Lebanese, and Syrians, the peoples of these two cities make up a very cosmopolitan urban population that reflects much of the diversity found throughout Brazil. But each city has its own unique mix of peoples that make for interesting contrasts.

The locals in Rio are often referred to as the *cariocas*, a term reflecting the easygoing, fun-loving nature of Rio's many self-possessed "beautiful people" who enjoy the good life of beaches, music, drink, and dance. The life of the *cariocas* is often stereotyped on the beaches of Copacabana and Ipanema and in the festive street parade marking the annual Carnival. To the *cariocas*, Rio represents the good life, a life that is to be enjoyed pursuing the many beachfront and evening entertainment pleasures of this vibrant city. The *cariocas* play hard and work some, but their emphasis is definitely on the play side of life. The residents of São Paulo, known as the *paulistinos*, also see themselves as the "beautiful people" but of a different class and orientation. This sprawling business and industrial city is Brazil's true melting pot of Asian and European immigrants. A disproportionate number of Japanese, Italians, Germans, Russians, Armenians, Lebanese, Syrians, and Jews have settled in São Paulo. They operate many of the city's major businesses and shops as well as patronize Brazil's many excellent ethnic and international restaurants. Unlike the more playful *cariocas* of Rio, the *paulistinos* tend to be more work-oriented. Representing greater wealth, class, and international sophistication, they take shopping and dining more seriously than the *cariocas*. Visitors to São Paulo are often surprised to discover how busy and European and North American this South American city is in comparison to more resort-oriented Rio.

LANGUAGE

Language can present difficulties for many visitors. Like the rest of Brazil, the peoples of Rio and São Paulo speak the mother colonial tongue – Portuguese. While some people speak Spanish and English, most do not. Therefore, you are well advised to take a small English-Portuguese dictionary with you to deal with many language situations requiring translation of terms as well as become somewhat animated in using sign language. A map and compass will also come in handy so you can resolve many directional problems on your own.

However, the language barrier is not as formidable as it may initially appear. Most personnel at hotel front desks speak some English. Be sure to ask them for assistance with names and addresses. Most will be happy to write out destinations in Portuguese to give to taxi drivers. Many shop owners speak some English or they will be able to understand you if you use a combination of sign language and sufficient pointing. Restaurant menus can be confusing, whether in Portuguese or Italian. Ask your waiter for assistance in translating menu items into English or Spanish, if that is a language option.

As independent travelers, who do not speak Portuguese nor much Spanish, we encounter few problems with language that cannot be resolved within a few minutes by finding someone who can speak English, using sign language, or getting by with an English-Portuguese dictionary. Best of all, coping with the language challenge provides some great opportunities to meet many friendly and helpful local people. Indeed, you'll seldom feel lost for long because of language problems.

TIME

Brazil has several time zones. However, Rio and São Paulo are two hours ahead of New York. If, for example, it's 12noon in Rio, it's 10am in New York. This also means that these cities are three hours behind Greenwich Mean Time (GMT). When it's 12noon in London, it's 9am in Rio and São Paulo. Consequently, few North Americans and Europeans experience jet lag when traveling to these cities. If you have difficulty with the time differences, you may want to visit these two websites: *www.timezoneconverter.com* and *www.worldtimeserver.com*.

SAFETY AND SECURITY

Rio and São Paulo are relatively safe cities as long as you take certain travel precautions. Since these cities have reputations for pickpockets, it's best to be somewhat paranoid about your possessions, especially your passport, money, and camera. Many of these thieves are children who operate in gangs – one distracts you by asking for money while others get your purse, wallet, camera, or bag from behind. Be very cautious with your purse and wallet – hold them very close and with a firm grip. Keep your valuables – including your money and passport – in safe places, such as your hotel safe or in a money belt. It's always a good idea to carry a photocopy of essential passport information – front info and stamped visa page – as well as traveler's check receipts separate from the originals.

In recent years Rio has developed a reputation for petty thievery, assaults, and pickpockets. Local authorities, however, have clamped down on such crime in tourist areas, especially near the beaches, major sightseeing attractions, and markets where you will see many policemen patrolling. Since buses tend to be crowded and have a reputation for being centers for skilled pickpockets and purse snatchers, it's best to avoid them. Also, avoid wandering into poor neighborhoods on your own, especially the *favelas*, which have reputations as centers for criminal activity; if you want to get up close and personal to such shantytowns, take the popular group tour in Rio (Favela Tour, Tel. 322-2727) instead.

Getting There

Rio and São Paulo are serviced by several international airlines as well as a convenient domestic shuttle between Rio and São Paulo. Direct flights from North America originate in Chicago, Houston, Los Angeles, Miami, New York City, and Toronto. Direct flights also originate in London. U.S. carriers servicing these two cities include American, United, Continental, Delta, and Air Canada. Brazil's major national carriers, Varig, TAM, and Transbrasil, also provide connections from major cities in North America. Varig, Brazil's largest airline, generally has a good record for safety and excellent service. They also are members of Star Alliance and co-share with United Airlines. For information on this airline's international and domestic services, including how to purchase discounted tickets online, visit their website (*www.varig.com.br/english*) or in North America call 1-800-468-2744.

❏ Since these cities have reputations for pickpockets, it's best to be somewhat paranoid about your possessions.

❏ Connections between Rio and São Paulo are very convenient if you use Varig's shuttle which departs every 15 to 30 minutes.

❏ Transportation is relatively inexpensive, if you use taxis and the subway or metrô.

❏ Avoid renting a car in the cities because traffic and parking are most inconvenient.

❏ Crowded buses can be inconvenient and unsafe – especially if you encounter pickpockets.

Connections between Rio and São Paulo are very convenient if you use Varig's shuttle, the Ponte Aérea (Air Bridge), which also operates Rio Sul and Nordeste. It departs every 30 minutes, from 6am to 10:30pm, with 15 minute intervals during the peak morning and evening rush hours. You do not need reservations. Just show up at the airport at least an hour before your planned departure time and hopefully you'll be able to get a seat. Early birds are more likely to get a seat at their preferred departure time. At press time these flights cost $147 one-way or $295 roundtrip (tickets are less expensive if purchased in Brazil). Best of all, they are efficiently run and depart right at the scheduled time – one of the most impressive airline operations we have encountered anywhere. The flight between Rio and São Paulo takes about 45 minutes.

Varig Airlines also offers a special domestic "Brazil Air Pass" which is a very good deal if you plan to visit five cities over a 21-day period. The cost is $530 which gives you five coupons to be used over that time period. If you wish to add more cities, you can do so at $100 per additional coupon.

The international airports charge a R$69.50 (US$32.63) departure tax which can be paid in either *reais* or US dollars. First class domestic airports charge a R$9.50 departure tax.

GETTING AROUND WITH EASE

Getting to and from airports is most convenient by taxis which are readily available and cost from $20 to $40 a ride, depending on your destination. Airports also are serviced by buses, which are less expensive as well as less inconvenient than taxis.

Transportation within Rio and São Paulo is relatively safe, convenient, and inexpensive, if you use taxis and the subway or metrô. We do not recommend renting a car for transportation within the cities because the traffic and parking situations are most inconvenient. However, you may want to rent a car for visiting areas outside Rio and São Paulo, especially the colonial and shopping towns of Itu and Embu near São Paulo. The outlying road system is very good and driving outside the cities is relatively safe; it's also a good way to see the countryside and enjoy a leisurely day beyond the hustle and bustle of the cities.

While both cities are served by an extensive bus system, you may want to forego the crowded buses which can be inconvenient and unsafe, especially if you encounter local pickpockets, who are known to prey on tourists.

INTERNATIONAL GROUP TOURS

Many visitors to Brazil come with a group. Numerous companies offer a wide variety of interesting package tours, with special emphasis on ecotourism, that include Rio and São Paulo along with trips to the Amazon, Iguaçu Falls, Bahia, Recife, and Brasilia. Since Rio and São Paulo are Brazil's two major international gateway cities, you will inevitably pass through one (usually Rio) or both of these cities on most group tours. Some of the major North American tour operators for Brazil include:

- **Anglatin Ltd.:** 132 E. Broadway, Suite 218, Eugene, OR 97401, Tel: 541-344-7023 or Fax: 541-344-7119. Email: anglatin@anglatin.com. Website: *www.anglatin.com*

- **Brazil Reservation System:** 1050 Edison Street, #c2, Santa Ynez, CA 93460. Tel. 1-800-544-5503 or Fax: 805-688-1021. Email: brazil@syv.com. Website: *www.brazilres. com*

- **Brazil Fiesta Tours:** 323 Geary Street, Suite 701, San Francisco, CA 94102. Tel. 1-800-200-0582 or Fax: 415-986-3029. Email: travel@brazilfiesta.com. Website: *www.brazilfiesta.com*

- **Brazil Nuts:** 1854 Trade Center Way, Suite 101B, Naples, FL 34109, Tel. 1-800-553-9959 or Fax 941-593-0267. Email: dot@brazilnuts.com. Website: *www.brazilnuts.com*

- **Brendan Tours:** 15137 Califa Street, Van Nuys, CA 91411, Tel. 1-800-421-8446 or Fax 818-902-9876. Email: info@brendantours.com. Website: *www.brendantours.com*

- **Escape Tours:** 1127 Pine Street, Suite 200, Seattle, WA 98101. Tel: 206-628-8687 or Fax: 206-628-3509. Email: ndikmen@webtravel.com. Website: *www.webtravel.com*

- **Festival Tours, Inc.:** 737 W. Oak Ridge Rd., Orlando, FL 32809, Tel: 407-850-0680 or Fax: 407-240-1480. Email: festour@bellsouth.net. Website: *www.festivaltours.com*

- **Latour:** 630 3rd Avenue, New York, NY 10017. Tel. 1-800-825-0825 or Fax 212-370-4007. Email: Reservations@latour.com. Website: *www.latour.com*

- **Maxim Tours Ltd.:** 50 Cutler St., Morristown, NJ 07960. Tel. 1-800-655-0222 or Fax: 973-984-5383. Email: maxim tours@earthlink.net. Website: *www.maximtours.com*

- **South Star Tours, Inc.:** 302 West Grand Avenue, Suite 8, El Segundo, CA 90245, Tel. 1-800-654-4468 or Fax: 310-416-8703. Email: sstartours@aol.com. Website: *www.southstartours.com*

For tour operators in the United Kingdom, visit the Brazilian Embassy site in London: *www.brazil.org.uk*. Also, check out the ads in *International Travel News*: *www.intltravelnews.com*.

LOCAL TRAVEL AGENCIES

You'll have no problem arranging tours once you arrive in Rio and São Paulo. Numerous travel agencies operate in these cities. Most offer regularly scheduled half-day city tours and night tours (dinner and samba) as well as customized day tours. They can provide cars, drivers, and guides to meet your individual needs. However, since both cities are relatively easy to do on your own, and getting around by taxi and subway is relatively easy and inexpensive, you may want to spend the first day or two in these cities exploring them on your own. Armed with this and other guidebooks, maps, a compass, and a sense of adventure, you should have little difficulty getting around these cities on your own. However, you may want to take advantage of certain specialty tours, such as the popular Favela Tour in Rio, which is difficult and inadvisable to do on your own.

ON-LINE TRAVEL DEALS

If you use the Internet, you can easily make airline, hotel, and car rental reservations on-line by using several on-line booking groups. The four major reservation services are:

>*www.expedia.com*   *www.priceline.com*
>*www.travelocity.com* *www.hotwire.com*

Other popular on-line reservation services, with many claiming discount pricing, include:

>*www.air4less.com*   *www.moments-notice.com*
>*www.airdeals.com*   *www.onetravel.com*
>*www.air-fare.com*   *www.site59.com*
>*www.bestfares.com*   *www.smarterliving.com*
>*www.biztravel.com*   *www.thetrip.com*
>*www.cheaptickets.com*   *www.travelhub.com*
>*www.concierge.com*   *www.travelscape.com*
>*www.etnlinks.com*   *www.travelzoo.com*
>*www.lowestfare.com*

However, while these on-line booking operations may appear to be convenient, we've found many of them can be more expensive than using a travel agent. This is especially true in the case of airline tickets. You'll often get the best airline rates through consolidators, which may be 30 to 40 percent less than the major on-line ticketing operations. Consolidators usually have small box ads in the Sunday travel sections of the **New York Times**, **Washington Post**, **Los Angeles Times**, and other major newspapers. Some of them, such as International Discount Travel, also provide price quotes on the Internet: ***www.idttravel.com***. Other popular consolidators specializing in discount ticketing include TicketPlanet (1-800-799-8888, ***www.ticketplanet.com***), Airtreks. com (1-800-350-0612, ***www.air-treks.com***), Air Brokers International (1-800-883-3273, *www.airbrokers.com*), International Airline Consolidators (1-800-305-6536, *www.intl-air-consolidators.com*), and World Travellers' Club (1-800-693-0411). If you're in a gambling mood, try these two "reverse auction" sites that allow you to set the price in the hopes that the company will make your dream price come true: *www.priceline.com* and *www.hotwire.com*. Make certain you are aware of any restrictions, such as departure and return dates, before you book.

CUSTOMS AT HOME

It's always good to know your country's Customs regulations before leaving home. Except for duty-free liquor, cigarettes, perfumes, and a few consumables, most Customs operations are not shopper-friendly. Indeed, traveler-shoppers are treated as major revenue streams for having engaged in shopping abroad. We are not particularly sympathetic to such discriminatory operations, however legal.

If, for example, you are a U.S. citizen planning to travel abroad, the United States Customs Service provides several helpful publications which are available free of charge from your nearest U.S. Customs Office (or write P.O. Box 7407, Washington, DC 20044). Several also are available in the "Traveler Information" section of the U.S. Customs website, *www.customs.ustreas.gov/travel*.

- *Know Before You Go* (Publication #512): Outlines facts about exemptions, mailing gifts, duty-free articles, as well as prohibited and restricted articles. Original art purchased in Brazil should enter the U.S. duty-free, as should items over 100 years old with proper documentation. However, most other items, especially jewelry, will be dutiable. The U.S. ostensibly prohibits the importation of pre-Columbian art from certain countries. However, dealers in such art should know what countries are affected and how to get legal art into the U.S. hassle-free.

- *International Mail Imports* answers many questions regarding mailing items from foreign countries back to the US. The U.S. Postal Service sends packages to Customs for examination and assessment of duty before they are delivered to the addressee. Some items are free of duty and some are dutiable. The rules have changed on mail imports, so do check on this before you leave the U.S.

- *GSP and the Traveler* itemizes goods from particular countries that can enter the U.S. duty-free. GSP regulations, which are designed to promote the economic development of certain Third World countries, permit many products, especially arts and handicrafts, to enter the United States duty-free, but only if GSP is currently in effect. If not, U.S. citizens will need to pay duty as well as complete a form that would refund the duties once GSP goes into effect again and is made retroactive – one of the U.S. Congress's annual budgetary rituals that is inconvenient to travelers and costly for taxpayers. Most items purchased in Brazil should be allowed to enter duty-free when GSP is operating. Do check on this before you leave the U.S. so you won't be surprised after you make your purchases in Brazil.

U.S. citizens may bring into the U.S. $400 worth of goods free of U.S. taxes every 30 days; the next $1,000 is subject to a flat 10 percent tax. Goods beyond $1,400 are assessed duty at varying rates applied to different classes of goods. Original works of art may enter the U.S. duty free as do items over 100 years old. You may be asked to provide documentation as to the age of an item you claim is an antique. If you are in Brazil and uncertain about U.S. duties on particular items, contact the U.S. Embassy in Brasilia or U.S. consulates in other cities and ask for local U.S. Customs assistance.

CURRENCY AND EXCHANGE RATES

The Brazilian unit of currency is the *real* (singular) or *reais* (plural or sometimes printed as *reals*). As we went to press in April 2001, the exchange rate between the Brazilian and the U.S. dollar was US$1 to R$2.13. The *real* (R$) is divided into 100 *centavos* (¢). Bank notes are issued in different colors and in denominations of 1, 5, 10, 50, and 100 *reais*. Coinage comes in 1, 5, 10, 25, and 50 *centavos*. To check on the latest exchange rates for various currencies relating to the *real*, visit these two currency converter websites:

www.oanda.com
www.xe.net/ucc

When it comes to money matters, you'll quickly discover that banks are not your friend. While you can change money at a few large banks that have exchange departments (*câmbio*), they are often inconvenient, close early (1-3pm), charge exchange fees, and are a bit scary with multiple security points and heavily armed guards. It's more convenient to exchange money at your hotel, although the exchange rate may be a little less favorable than the official bank rate. At some hotels the exchange rate will actually be better than at the bank. When you arrive at the international airports, personnel at the taxi stands will often exchange US dollars at a more favorable rate than the bank found in the airport. Both US banknotes and traveler's checks are acceptable, with preference for US banknotes. Many shops will accept US dollars as payment and you get more favorable prices by using US dollars. You also will find **ATMs** which accept either Visa or MasterCard. Our advice: avoid the banks, carry lots of US dollars (but carefully), and change your money at hotels.

Credit cards are now widely accepted throughout most major cities and towns in Brazil. Hotels, restaurants, and shops prefer Visa and MasterCard, although many will also accept American Express.

Brazil has a long history of inflation. Within the past two years the US dollar has become very strong against the *real*. Indeed, devaluation in 1999 saw the value of US dollar nearly double in Brazil. Consequently, today Brazil remains a good travel and shopping buy for U.S. citizens. Whatever you do, don't exchange a lot of US dollars into *real*.

ELECTRICITY AND WATER

Since electrical current is not uniform throughout Brazil, be cautious when using appliances with specific voltage requirements. Electricity in both Rio and São Paulo is 110 or 120 volts, 60 cycles alternative current (AC), the same as in the U.S. and Canada. Elsewhere in the country it can be 220 volts (Recife and Brasília) and even 127 volts (Manaus and Salvador). If you are traveling to places outside Rio and São Paulo, be sure to check on the local electrical current before using appliances requiring either 110 or 220 volts. Plug configurations for electrical wall outlets are relatively uniform – they take plugs with two round prongs, the same as in many parts of Europe. You may need to pack an electrical adapter if your appliances take a flat plug.

Tap water is not safe to drink in Brazil. Hotels and restaurants usually provide bottled water. You can purchase inexpensive bottled water in many small neighborhood markets.

HEALTH AND INSURANCE

You should have few if any health problems in Rio and São Paulo as long at you take normal eating and drinking precautions. Drink only bottled water and other bottled drinks, avoid ice, and stay clear of uncooked street vendor foods. If you do encounter a health problem, it will most likely be diarrhea, which can be treated with a few good over-the-counter remedies such as Imodium. Medications, as well as free medical advice, are readily dispensed at pharmacies (*farmácias*) which are conveniently found throughout the cities.

AIDS is a major problem in Brazil, with a disproportionate number of HIV-positive cases found in Rio and São Paulo. Consequently, avoid any behaviors that might put you in contact with HIV carriers or contaminated blood. If you require major medical assistance, such as hospitalization, you may be wise to be evacuated home. Brazil is not known for having particularly good health care facilities.

You should consider taking out a special insurance policy when traveling to Brazil to cover situations not covered by your medical, home, auto, and personal insurance back home. For example, most insurance does not cover treatment for illnesses or accidents while traveling outside your home country. Therefore, you should consider acquiring evacuation insurance in case serious illness or injuries would require that you be evacuated home through special transportation and health care arrangements. Many companies offer evacuation insurance. One of the best kept travel secrets for acquiring inexpensive evacuation insurance is to become a member of DAN (Divers Alert Network). In the U.S., call 1-800-446-2671 (The Peter B. Bennett Center, 6 West Colony Place, Durham, NC 27705; website: *www.diversalertnetwork.org*). Without such insurance, special evacuation arrangements could cost between US$10,000 and US$20,000! If you are into adventure travel and plan to engage in physically challenging activities, health and evacuation insurance should be on your "must do" list before departing for Brazil.

The following websites will connect you to several companies that offer special insurance for travelers:

www.worldtravelcenter.com
www.globaltravelinsurance.com
www.travelinsurance.com
www.travelex.com
www.etravelprotection.com

www.travelguard.com
www.travelsecure.com
www.travelprotect.com
www.globalcover.com

DINING

Both Rio and São Paulo are wonderful places for sampling local and international cuisines as well as engaging in one of travelers' great pastimes – lifestyle shopping, a combination of shopping *and* dining, especially at lunch time (1-3pm) when you can wile the afternoon away with food, drink, conversation, and strategizing the rest of your quickly disappearing day. From traditional Brazilian restaurants, with their grilled meats and buffets, to Italian, French, Portuguese, Spanish, Japanese, Indian, and Lebanese restaurants, these cities offer a wide range of dining choices. São Paulo boasts the best selection of restaurants in the country, with more than 12,000 restaurants representing 36 different cuisines.

❑ Banks are not your best friend for exchanging money. It's often more convenient to exchange money at hotels where the exchange rate may be higher than at the bank.

❑ Electrical current is not uniform throughout Brazil, but it is 110 or 120 volts in Rio and São Paulo.

❑ Few restaurants offer menus in English. If you can't decipher the dishes, ask your waiter for assistance.

❑ Many restaurants serve huge portions which can easily be shared between two people.

❑ Dining usually takes place late in the day – lunch after 1pm and dinner after 9pm.

Brazilian dining establishments come in many different forms, from inexpensive street vendors (best to avoid because of potential health problems), fast food outlets, and *lanchonetes* – a kind of bar/café combination where you can get snacks, coffee, soft drinks, and beer – to more pricey local and international restaurants. Most dining is very casual, with smart casual dress acceptable even in top restaurants.

Brazilian cuisine tends to be very regional – representing four major regions: *comida mineria* from Minas Gerais; *comida baiana* from the Salvador coast; *comida do sertão* from the Northeast; and *comida gaúcha* from Rio Grande do Sul.

If you want to sample a traditional Brazilian dish, which is ubiquitous in local restaurants and comes closest to being a national dish, try the *feijoada*. Not a particularly pretty dish, it's a tasty soupy mixture of black beans, pork, sausage, and smoked meat cooked with garlic. Wednesdays and Saturdays are popular *feijoada* days – for both lunch and dinner – in many restaurants.

Brazilian restaurants called *churrascarias* serve a variety of grilled meats cut from huge spits that constantly arrive at your table – a kind of reverse buffet complete with roving waiters and a clever table signaling system.

While restaurant dining can become expensive, especially if you dine at the top establishments, you'll find many inexpensive dining alternatives, such as *padarias* (bakeries) and *lanchonetes*, and special menus. Many *lanchonetes* and restaurants offer less expensive alternatives to their main menu items. If it's not posted, ask if they have a *prato feito*, *sortido*, or *prato comercial*.

Many restaurants have a *couvert* charge. This is a charge for some initial table food (*couberto*) – raw carrots, olives, cheese, quail eggs – which automatically appears when you sit down. Unless you tell your waiter not to bring this item, you will pay for it whether or not you want it – an irritating charge for people not used to this type of automatic add-on. The *couvert* charge can run from R$2 to R$13 per person, depending on the restaurant. Also, watch out for other pricey items which you may not be prepared for unless you ask. Bottled water, which is the only restaurant water you should drink, can be expensive compared to other types of drinks. Imported wines also can be very expensive. Less expensive local wines are available but they are not the same quality as the imported wines.

Few restaurants offer menus in English. If you can't decipher the dishes, ask your waiter for assistance. There is usually someone who can translate the menu or at least give you advice on what is especially good. If not volunteered, we often ask the question *"What's especially good at this restaurant – dishes that keep bring back the crowds?"* with surprisingly good results!

Many restaurants serve huge portions which can easily be shared among two or three people. Check on the portions before ordering since you may want to share a dish with someone else in your party. Ordering one dish and an extra plate for two people is acceptable restaurant etiquette. Many restaurants also will give you doggy bags (ask for an *embalagem*).

For many locals, lunch is the main meal for the day. Since breakfast is not particularly popular, don't expect to find many places serving breakfast outside your hotel. Your best choices for breakfast would be a *padarias* (bakery) or *lanchonete* (bar/café combination).

Dining usually takes place later in the day than more visitors anticipate. Lunch starts around 1pm and may go until 3pm. Dinner usually starts after 9pm and really gets going around 10pm. If you arrive before 8pm, you will most likely be the only one in the restaurant. Reservations are always recommended.

Most restaurants add a 10 percent service charge. However,

waiters still expect an additional tip since the service charge does not necessarily go to them.

ACCOMMODATIONS

Both Rio and São Paulo boast some of the best accommodations in all of Brazil. Four- and five-star hotels abound in these two cities. They include such classic hotels as the beachfront Copacabana Palace Hotel (an Orient-Express property) and the Caesar Park in Rio and the L'Hotel São Paulo and Maksoud Plaza, two of São Paulo' s very best hotels. Room rates can run from US$150 to US400 a night. You'll also find many one-, two- and three-star hotels with rates ranging from US$25 to US$100 a night. During the off-season, many hotels discount their rates by 25-35 percent. Since many hotels also include breakfast with the room rate, be sure to check on whether or not it's included in the rate. Many hotels add a 10 percent service charge plus five percent tax to the bill.

If you plan to visit Rio and São Paulo during the annual Carnival time (February or March), be sure to make room reservations well in advance – 10 months ahead of time would not be too early for choice properties. For quick Internet access to the major hotels in Rio and São Paulo, visit the hotel section of the Brazilian National Tourist Board (EMBRATUR) available through the website of the Brazilian Embassy in London:

www.brazil.org.uk

BUSINESS HOURS

Most **business offices** are open Monday to Friday, 9am - 6pm. **Banks** are open Monday to Friday, 10am - 4pm. Most **shops** are open Monday to Friday, 9am - 6pm, and on Saturday, 9am to 1pm or 2pm. Most large **shopping centers** are open Monday to Friday, 10am - 10pm and on Saturday, 10am - 8pm; however, some shops within these centers may open later or close earlier. Hours for **weekend markets** will vary depending on the particular market. Some are only open on Saturday whereas others only open on Sunday; a few are open on both Saturday and Sunday. Market hours tend to be from 8am or 9am to 5pm or 6pm. A few open later and close earlier.

We recommend doing most of your downtown and shopping center shopping during the weekdays and evenings. Keep your weekends free for exploring the many markets both within and outside the cities.

ANTICIPATED COSTS

Rio and São Paulo can be expensive places to visit if you decide to visit these cities in style. After all, they are major cities that offer the best of the best in accommodations, restaurants, and shopping. At the same time, you will often find many good value specials for visiting Rio during the off season. These specials include round-trip air transportation, hotels, and transfers, with many trips originating from New York City, Miami, and Los Angeles in the United States. You can easily find their specials in ads that appear in the travel sections of the Sunday newspapers in these gateway cities, or visit several of the websites identified earlier in this chapter

Many budget travelers manage to visit Rio and São Paulo on a shoestring by staying in inexpensive hotels, finding cheap eateries, and using inexpensive public transportation. The best sources for such class of travel include the following guidebooks which are designed specifically for budget travelers who are often long on time but short on cash: *Lonely Planet Brazil*, *Rough Guide to Brazil*, and *Footprint Brazil*. These guides are available in many major bookstores or through Impact's online bookstore (*www.impactpublications.com* or *www.ishoparoundtheworld.com*).

However, if you follow our many "best of the best" recommendations, you'll find Rio and São Paulo no more or less expensive than most other major international cities that offer quality travel and shopping. In fact, these two cities are now good buys because of the favorable exchange rate between the US dollar and the Brazilian *real*.

TIPPING

This is a tipping culture – tips are welcome by many people in the service industry. While restaurants normally add a 10 percent service charge (*taxa de serviço*) on your bill, waiters would appreciate another five percent, although it's really not necessary to include this extra tip (do so for exceptional service). If no service charge is included, leave a 10 percent tip. Porters should get R$2 (US$.50) per bag. Since taxis are metered and drivers do not expect tips, only pay the amount calculated on the meter; drivers do expect to be tipped R$1-2 for each bag handled. Hotel personnel, from doorman and concierge to chambermaids, expect to receive small tips. Barbers and hairdressers expect 10-15 percent tips. Other people expecting tips include shoeshine kids, guides, and beggars.

Who and how much you tip is up to you. Again, keep in

mind that most service personnel are paid very low wages. Two general rules to follow when tipping in Brazil:

1. **Carry lots of small change with you for small tips,** especially 1 and 5 *reais* banknotes and 25 and 50 *centavos* coins. Without adequate change you may end up either over-tipping with large bills or not tipping at all and thus earning the displeasure of people who deserve a tip.

2. **If you are going to tip, be sure to tip generously to the right people at the right time.** Timing is everything when tipping. Important people should be tipped early on and generously if you want to maximize their services. For example, tip your hotel doorman, porter, and room attendant for initial services received. Let them know you will be appreciating their future service. Don't decide to keep everyone guessing what you plan to give them when you leave. They may turn out to be your best friend for getting things you need, from extra service to information and advice on the city.

For additional advice on tipping practices, visit these two websites which include information on proper tipping behavior:

www.tipping.org
www.talesmag.com

TOURIST OFFICES

Government tourist information is not well organized nor widely available. To a very large extent, you are on your own in Rio and São Paulo with guidebooks and a few commercial maps and brochures you may acquire at tourist desks and bookstores in these cities.

Prior to arriving in Brazil, you may want to contact a Brazilian embassy or consulate nearest you. In the United States and Canada, these are found at the following locations:

Brazilian Embassy
3006 Massachusetts Ave., NW
Washington, DC 20008-3699
Tel. 202-238-2700 or Fax 202-238-2827
Website: *www.brasilemb.org*

Brazilian Consulate
401 North Michigan Avenue, Suite 3050
Chicago, IL 60611
Tel. 312-464-0245 or Fax 312-464-0299

Brazilian Consulate
1700 West Loop South, Suite 1450
Houston, TX 77027
Tel. 713-961-3063 or Fax 713-961-3070

Brazilian Consulate
8484 Wilshire Blvd., Suite 711/730
Beverly Hills, CA 90211-3216
Tel. 213-651-2664 or Fax 213-274-2601

Brazilian Consulate
2601 South Bay Shore Drive, Suite 800
Miami, FL 33133
Tel. 305-285-6200 or Fax 305-285-6232

Brazilian Consulate
630 Fifth Avenue, 20th Floor
New York, NY 10020
Tel. 212-489-7930 or Fax 212-956-3465

Brazilian Consulate
300 Montgomery Street, Suite 900
San Francisco, CA 941-04-1913
Tel. 415-981-8170 or Fax 415-981-3628

In the case of Rio, be sure to contact RIOTUR, the City of Rio
de Janeiro Tourism Authority: *www.rio.rj.gov.br/riotur* and
www.destinationrio.com. See page 113 for contact information in
the United States.

Once you arrive at the airports in Rio or São Paulo, check at
the local tourist information desks for maps, booklets, and
assistance with any of your travel questions. The personnel at
these desk can usually help with hotel reservations. These desks
are located near the taxi and car rental areas.

USEFUL WEBSITES

The Internet is slowly coming to Brazil. For now, there are few
really useful websites for accessing travel-related information on
Rio and São Paulo. Hotels, especially those affiliated with

international chains, are most likely to have Internet connections with home pages and email addresses. Very few shops have Internet connections, including email addresses. While this situation is likely to change dramatically over the next five years, for now the best ways to contact these places is by telephone, fax, and mail.

Nonetheless, you will find a few websites that provide useful information on travel to Brazil. One of the best such sites, with good linkages to hotels in Rio and São Paulo, is operated by the Brazilian National Tourist Board (EMBRATUR – *www.embra tur.gov.br*) and is available through the Brazilian Embassy in London:

www.brazil.org.uk

Three of the best Brazilian sites actually focus only on the city of Rio de Janiero:

www.ipanema.com
www.destinationrio.com
www.rio.rj.gov.br/riotur

While São Paulo lacks comparable sites, visit the following sites for information on São Paulo:

www.sao-paulo.com
www.webguidesaopaulo.com

For linkages to tourism in Brazil, visit these two sites:

www.escapeartist.com/obrazil/brazil2.html
www.brazilinfo.net

For useful online travel guidebook treatments of Brazil, visit the Fodor's, Lonely Planet, and Rough Guides websites:

www.fodors.com
www.lonelyplanet.com
www.roughguide.com

For travel-shopping information related to this guidebook as well as several other countries, visit our new iShopAroundTheWorld website:

www.ishoparoundtheworld.com

Shopping Treasures and Rules For Success

W HILE SHOPPING IN RIO AND SÃO PAULO may initially look familiar to you, there are certain things you need to know about shopping in these cities which will make your shopping experience more rewarding. From encountering unique products to handling transactions, shipping, and customs, you should find shopping in Rio and São Paulo to be one of the highlights of your Brazilian travel adventure.

DISCOVER BRAZIL'S BEST PRODUCTS

The many shops and markets you'll encounter in Rio and São Paulo offer a wide range of attractive products. The major difference between the two cities will become immediately apparent as you shop their major shops and shopping centers: Rio is more oriented to the tourist market and less affluent local population than São Paulo which is more business-oriented, cosmopolitan, affluent, and stylish than Rio. Put another way, São Paulo is to New York what Rio is to New Orleans – two very different shopping styles and cultures. While we summarize each of the following products in the individual city chapters, in general you'll find these products to be the major shopping attractions:

❑ **Gems and jewelry:** Brazil is world famous for its gemstones and jewelry. Indeed, Brazil is the world's largest producer of colored gemstones and gold. The main Brazilian gems include emerald, aquamarine, tanzanite, amethyst, tourmaline, rubellite (red tourmaline), citrine, imperial topaz, blue topaz, and opal. Other gemstones, which may be used by local jewelers but are not found locally in any large deposits, include diamonds, chrysoberyl, garnet, chrysolite, ruby, sapphire, Alexandrite, Kunzite, and Morganite. One of the world's most famous vertically integrated jewelers (from prospecting, mining, cutting, and polishing to designing, wholesaling, and retailing), H. Stern, is headquartered in Rio and includes 85 retail outlets in Brazil and 90 more around the world. They, along with several other jewelry stores, offer excellent designed jewelry at competitive prices. If you want to get a real education on Brazilian gemstones and jewelry, be sure to visit H. Stern's headquarters shop, as well as its small but highly competitive neighbor, Amsterdam Sauer, along Rua Visconde de Pirajá in the Ipanema section of Rio, where you along with busloads of tourists will be given a highly enlightening tour of Brazil's gemstone and jewelry industry. You'll also find a some very nice and well priced fashion jewelry in both cities, but especially in Rio.

❑ São Paulo is to New York what Rio is to New Orleans – two different shopping styles and cultures.

❑ Brazil is the world's largest producer of colored gemstones and gold.

❑ São Paulo is Brazil's fashion capital. The trendy locals here are more fashion conscious than their leisure-oriented counterparts in Rio.

❑ The main art scene is found in São Paulo, although Rio also has some interesting galleries.

❑ Rio is the center for Brazilian antiques and collectibles; São Paulo is oriented to European antiques and design.

❑ **Clothes, shoes, and accessories:** Local residents, especially young people, shop a great deal for trendy clothes and accessories. Indeed, many shopping malls are primarily centers for clothing, shoe, and accessory shops. Clothes range from stylish and skimpy beachwear in Rio to designer boutiques and fashionable smart casual business attire in the trendy shops of São Paulo. In fact, São Paulo is Brazil's fashion capital with a disproportionate number of local clothing designers, many of whom have their own boutiques integrated with designer label clothing lines from Europe and the United States. Given São Paulo's business and international orientation, local residents there tend to be more fashion conscious than their more leisure-oriented counterparts in Rio. Also look for stylish and colorful handbags made from local leather and fiber products. Many of the weekend markets offer a wide range of inexpensive clothes, T-shirts, and leather goods.

❏ **Art:** Brazil has a very vibrant art scene with many galleries representing hundreds of Brazilian and international artists. The main art scene is found in São Paulo, although Rio also has some interesting galleries. Numerous art galleries in São Paulo represent Brazil's top artists as well as interact with the international art community, from New York City to London and Paris. In addition to visiting various established art galleries, look for special public and private exhibitions held at galleries, hotels, and universities.

❏ **Antiques and collectibles:** Antique collectors will have a great time shopping in Rio and São Paulo for everything from unique colonial furniture and glassware to jewelry, silver, ceramics, and small collectibles. Rio is the center for Brazilian antiques and collectibles with many shops, shopping centers, and markets offering a wide range of varying quality antiques and collectibles. São Paulo's antique shops represent more European antiques, especially furniture and accessories, and are more oriented to home decorating and professional designer work than Rio's more collector-type antique shops. Indeed, most of Brazil's major designers are found in São Paulo. You'll immediately see the difference in quality and style once you visit a few of São Paulo's top antique and home decorative shops.

❏ **Tribal art and antiquities:** A few shops in both Rio and São Paulo specialize in tribal artifacts from Brazil's more than 70 indigenous tribes. Ranging from colorful feathered headdresses and armbands to carved utensils, weapons, and ceremonial pieces, many are newly commissioned pieces, although you may occasionally find a older collector's item. The prices tend to be moderate to expensive, although reasonable compared to comparable indigenous artifacts found in many other countries. You'll occasionally come across excellent quality Indian antiquities uncovered from excavations in Peru and elsewhere in Latin America. One shop in São Paulo specializes in these antiquities – a fabulous one-stop shop for pre-Columbian antiquities!

❑ **Handicrafts, gifts, and souvenirs:** There seems to be no end to the variety of handicrafts and souvenirs found in the shops and markets of Rio and São Paulo – carved bowls, masks, wooden saints, hammocks, lace, T-shirts, wall hangings, toys, stuffed animals, throw pillows, ceramics, geodes, sand paintings, candles, watercolors, oil paintings, prints, rugs, pottery, baskets, agate sculptured birds, and clay figurines. You'll find a full range of varying quality handicrafts, from true tourist kitsch to good quality folk art and crafts.

❑ **Music:** One of the nicest souvenirs from Brazil is a sampling of its unique and interesting music. Indeed, Brazil has its own beats, from popular MPB (Música Popular Brasileira) and samba-canção to bossa-nova, chorinho, pagode, tropi-calistes, jazz, Afro-beat, and other interesting musical combinations. Numerous music shops offer a full range of Brazilian music on both CDs and tapes. You'll occasionally meet talented street musicians at the weekend markets who also sell their own CDs at very reasonable prices (US$3-5).

TAKE KEY SHOPPING INFORMATION

Depending on what you plan to buy, you should take all the necessary information you need to make informed shopping decisions. Do your shopping research and documentation *before* you leave home. Shops in Brazil are not good places to get an expensive education. For example, even though some shops will tell you their gemstones and jewelry are 20 percent less than what you can buy them for back home, don't believe them unless you have documentation and know qualitative differences. Some jewelry shops in Rio, for example, offer mediocre gemstones which an educated eye can immediately see, even though the shop may make all kinds of exaggerated claims about offering "the best of the best." After all, you don't want to end up purchasing an emerald ring or aquamarine stone in Rio and then discover you can get the same item back home for much less. If you are looking for antiques and home furnishings, especially furniture, include with your "wish list" room measurements to help you determine if particular items will fit into your home. You might take photographs with you of particular rooms you hope to furnish.

If you plan to shop for clothes and accessories, especially leather goods such as shoes and handbags, your homework should include taking an inventory of your closets and identifying particular colors, fabrics, and designs you wish to acquire to complement and enlarge your present wardrobe. Good quality clothes, shoes, and handbags made in Brazil can be good buys two thirds of what you may pay back home. At the same time, many shoes and handbags come in very interesting, and at times unusual, colors. Much of the clothing for women is styled to emphasize bust and derrière to a far greater extent than clothing in the U.S. Even the jeans seem to fit differently! Be sure you know what colors work best for your wardrobe. Top quality imported designer-label clothes and accessories (mainly from Italy and France) will probably be more expensive than similar items found in department stores and boutiques back home. However, you may find a style unavailable in stores at home. If you are from the U.S., you should look at comparable selections found at the top department stores, such as Saks Fifth Avenue, Nordstrom, and Neiman Marcus. This means visiting their designer-label and couture sections for comparable quality and prices. Since you will see lots of shoes, handbags, and other leather goods in Rio and São Paulo – many being knock-off designs of Italian and French designer-labels – you may want to prepare yourself for such items.

❑ Take with you measurements and photographs of rooms that could become candidates for home decorative items.

❑ Be sure to take information on any particular clothes, accessories, or jewelry (sizes, colors, comparative prices) with you to look for or have made when in Brazil.

❑ Do comparative shopping before arriving in Brazil.

❑ Half the fun of shopping while traveling in Brazil is the serendipity of discovering the unique and exotic.

DO COMPARATIVE SHOPPING

You should do comparative shopping both at home and within Brazil in order to get a good idea of what is or is not a good buy. Our rule of thumb is that if a comparable item can be found at home, and it is not at least 20 percent cheaper buying it abroad, it's probably not worth the effort of buying it abroad for such a small savings. This is especially true in the case of gemstones and jewelry where it's usually "buyer beware" when dealing with such issues as authenticity, quality, and pricing. After all, back home you most likely will have return privileges, and you may be protected by consumer protection regulations or you can take legal action should such items be misrepresented.

While you should do comparison shopping before you leave home, once you arrive in Brazil, the only comparisons you can make are between various shops and products you encounter. You'll never know if you are getting a good deal unless you have done your shopping homework beforehand.

The first step in doing comparative shopping starts at home. Determine exactly what you want and need. Make lists. As you compile your list, spend some time "window shopping" in the local stores, examining catalogs, telephoning for information, and checking Internet shopping sites such as *www.novica.com* and *www.eziba.com*.

Once you arrive in Rio and São Paulo, your shopping plans will probably change considerably as you encounter many new items you had not planned to purchase but which attract your interest and buying attention. Indeed, half the fun of shopping while traveling in these two cities is the serendipity of discovering the unique and exotic – an amethyst necklace, a beautiful contemporary oil painting, intriguing bronze sculptures, darling stuffed toys, colorful carved folk art, feathered tribal ceremonial artifacts, a beautifully crafted leather handbag, an antique colonial religious figure, an 18th century Spanish desk, and designer shoes – things you could not have anticipated encountering but which you now see, feel, and judge as possible acquisitions for your home and wardrobe. These are the great shopping moments that require local knowledge about differences in quality and pricing. Many products, such as paintings, pottery, or jewelry, may be unique one-of-a-kind items that are difficult to compare. You must judge them in terms of their designs, colors, and intrinsic value. Other items, such as fashion jewelry, gemstones, leather handbags, and souvenir items will beg comparative shopping because the same or similar quality items are widely available in numerous shops and factories.

You'll have plenty of opportunities to do comparison shopping in Rio and São Paulo. You are well advised to visit several shops soon after your arrival in order to get some sense of market prices for various items you are likely to frequently encounter, especially jewelry, gemstones, leather goods, and handicrafts. In Rio, you should initially visit several shops in the São Conrado Fashion Mall and Forum de Ipanema as well as the highly competitive jewelry giants H. Stern and Amsterdam Sauer in downtown Ipanema (next to each other on Rua Visconde de Pirajá). In São Paulo, immediately head for the city's shopping mecca – Cerqueiras César and the Jardins, especially the many shops along Rua Oscar Freire, Rua Peixoto Gomide, Rua Augusta, and Rua Bela Cintra.

KEEP TRACK OF RECEIPTS

It's important to keep track of all of your purchases for making an accurate Customs declaration. Be sure to ask for receipts wherever you shop. If a shop doesn't issue receipts, ask them to create a receipt by writing the information on a piece of paper, include the shop's name and address, and sign it.

Since it's so easy to misplace receipts, you might want to organize your receipts using a form similar to the following example. Staple a sheet or two of notebook or accountant's paper to the front of a large manila envelope and number down the left side of the page. Draw one or two vertical columns down the right side. Each evening, sort through that day's purchases, write a description including style and color of the purchase on the accompanying receipt, and enter that item on your receipt record. Record the receipt so later you'll know exactly which item belongs to the receipt – especially if the receipt is written in Portuguese!

CUSTOMS DECLARATION RECORD FORM

Receipt #	Item	Price (R$1)	Price (US$)
1. 42119	Amethyst ring	R$3850	$1807.51
2.			
3.			
4.			

Put the receipts in the manila envelope and pack the purchases away. If you're missing a receipt, make a note of it beside the appropriate entry.

4 | SHOPPING RULES FOR SUCCESS

Many people may initially be drawn to Brazil because of Rio's beaches, but they soon discover one of the great pleasures of visiting Brazil is its lifestyle shopping. Indeed, you'll find lots of interesting jewelry, gems, art, antiques, clothes, accessories, leather goods, and handicrafts to keep you busy shopping for several days. Add dining to your shopping sojourns and you'll think you've found one of the world's great travel adventures.

As you begin shopping in Rio and São Paulo, keep these basic "rules" in mind. We discovered them as we made our way through the many shopping centers, shops, and markets in Rio and São Paulo:

1. **Focus your initial shopping on the major shopping areas.** Most shopping areas are very well defined – shopping centers, major streets, and weekend markets. Similar quality shops, with similar products, tend to be located near each other, which is nice for doing comparative shopping.

2. **Expect to find the best quality shopping at the best quality locations.** It should come as no surprise that the best quality shopping is usually found in the top shopping centers, upscale shopping streets, and a few five-star hotels that include boutique shops. These places tend to screen the quality of shops that are allowed to rent their shop space. Shops in these areas also tend to cater to the tastes of upscale visitors. When in doubt where to shop for quality items, contact your hotel concierge or front desk for shopping recommendations. They usually know the best places to shop – as well as to dine – based upon positive feedback from their many guests.

3. **Look for a few out-of-the-way places for quality shopping.** Some of the best shopping will be found in studios, galleries, shops, and homes that are located outside the major shopping areas. If you learn of a shop that is excellent but located off the beaten path, it may be worth finding it – literally a diamond in the rough. Many of these places cater to an exclusive clientele rather than to walk-in traffic. Indeed, some of our best shopping in Rio and São Paulo has been with shops that are difficult to find.

4. **Expect to shop in two shopping cultures which require different shopping skills.** The first world is the most familiar one for visitors – shopping centers, street shops, department stores, and hotel shops that have window displays, well organized interiors, and fixed prices which may or may not be all that fixed, depending

on your ability to persuade shops to discount prices. Indeed, depending on the product and shop, you may be able to get a 20 percent discount – but only if you ask. The second shopping culture consists of traditional weekend markets, fairs, or bazaars consisting of vendor stalls, which tend to be somewhat chaotic and involve price uncertainty and bargaining skills. While prices may be ostensibly fixed amongst many vendors, you can often haggle over prices in these markets.

5. **Use US dollars for getting a price advantage.** When discussing prices, you'll usually get a better price if you deal in US dollars. Given the weak *real*, the US dollar tends to be the preferred hedge against inflation. Always deal in US dollars when shopping for gemstones. This is the traditional currency for buying such items.

6. **Get prices quoted in the local currency.** When given a choice between quoting a price in US dollars or Brazilian *real* (R$), ask for the *real* price. When it comes time to bargain over the price, shift from *real* to US dollars, which should put you in the most advantageous bargaining position.

7. **Take taxis to shops but don't ask them to wait.** Since taxis are metered and don't expect tips, just leave them once you get out of the taxi. When you need another taxi, you can usually flag down one on a busy street, or the shop can call one for you. It only takes five to 10 minutes for a radio taxi to arrive.

8. **Beware of free jewelry demonstrations with well lit and sparkling showrooms that cater to your new-found jewelry needs.** After completing the interesting factory tour, you will inevitably up in the not-too-free retail sales room with its bright lights, beautiful displays, and friendly salespeople who want to assist you with all your new-found jewelry needs (you probably did not have such needs a half-hour earlier). You may be pressured from a combination of the tour and sales person to make an impulse, and expensive, buy without first comparing prices and quality of gemstones and jewelry at other shops that do not have the overhead of the "free tour" and huge sales room. Our advice: Take the free tour to learn about Brazilian gemstones and jewelry, but tell yourself that you can always come back tomorrow –

after you have a clearer head and a chance to put your new "jewelry needs" in better perspective. However, now may be the best time to bargain for the lowest price the shop may offer.

9. **Ask about guarantees, return policies, and holding items**. If you're interested in an item but you're not sure if you want to buy it right now, ask the shop if they would be willing to put it "on hold" for at least 24 hours. Many shops will do this. Also, if you are interested in purchasing an expensive gem or piece of jewelry, ask about guarantees and return policies. Most large shops have written policies which are very consumer-friendly. Small shops may be a different story. If the shop can't guarantee an item and is unwilling to give you a money-back return within seven days, you should have second thoughts about purchasing the item. After all, you might discover tomorrow that you paid too much for the item or you find another item preferable to this purchase. In this case, ask to put the item "on hold" and continue looking around. Try to create as much flexibility as possible when purchasing any expensive items you have doubts about. Chances are your doubts may be confirmed.

10. **Be cautious of possible crime problems in shopping areas**. It's easy to let down your guard when shopping, especially in shopping centers and markets where you can easily become a victim of purse snatchers and pickpockets. Being paranoid is good when shopping.

11. **Look for best buys on Brazilian-made products**. Anything made with local labor content will tend to be a good buy given the relatively inexpensive cost of labor in Brazil. While you will find many imported goods in Rio and São Paulo – especially designer clothes, accessories, tableware, and gift items – expect to pay a premium for such items. Similar item will most likely be more expensive here than back home. Unless an item appears to be truly unique and thus difficult to find back home, we normally don't waste our time shopping for such items.

12. **Know your Customs regulations.** Don't be surprised to discover that ostensible savings on some purchases, such as gems and jewelry, will be negated by Customs

duties. Also, know what items are prohibited from being imported into your country. In some countries, prohibited items include foodstuffs and pre-Columbian art from certain countries. Much of the pre-Columbian art for sale in Brazil was excavated in other countries. Much of it comes from Peru.

13. **Check out the interiors of shops where you may find some hidden treasures.** Don't be turned off by initial window or first room appearances. Be sure to go deep into a shop, especially ask to see the backrooms or upstairs where the "good stuff" may be found. Items found in the windows or in the first room of a shop may not be representative of the shop's best inventory.

14. **Don't fall in love too early – not everything you see is necessarily for sale.** One of the real frustrations of shopping in Rio and São Paulo is to discover something you really love and then to be told that the item is not for sale – only for display or it belongs in the owner's personal collection. As you might expect, the items that are not for sale are usually the most attractive and best quality – the ones you are likely to fall in love with prematurely!

15. **Beware of shopping recommendations.** The best shopping recommendations will usually come from the concierges and front desk managers of top hotels – they often know where their best guests shop for such popular items as jewelry, gems, clothes, art, handicrafts, and antiques. They also know which shops generate complaints because of high prices, poor quality and service, and problems with shipping. Show them your map and ask them for their top three recommendations in different product categories. They will usually mark the shopping areas and shops on your map. Some of these people maintain a printed list of recommended shops by category which you should try to see. However, not all top hotels are so knowledgeable and helpful when it comes to shopping. It depends on the hotel and the services it provides for its guests. The worst people to ask for shopping recommendations are tour guides, drivers, touts, and general service personnel. They are either on "on the take" or have no sense of quality shopping. You may pay dearly for their advice!

16. **Arm yourself with a good map, compass, and a sense of adventure.** Shopping in Rio and São Paulo can be a great adventure it you plan it properly. Try to get a good map, which can be difficult to find, and take a compass with you for finding your bearings. Bookstores have better maps than the tourist offices, although getting a useful map still remains a challenge – a good reason to travel with a compass since your map may often fail you! H. Stern provides an "almost usable" free map of Rio.

17. **Always ask for receipts.** While many shops will automatically give you a sales receipt, others do not. Since you should keep a good record of your purchases for Customs, make sure the shop gives you a receipt. You also may need the receipt if you learn something is wrong with your purchase. When buying jewelry, be sure to ask for a certificate of authenticity.

18. **Take personal checks and cash when shopping.** While many shops accept Visa and MasterCard, and to a lesser extent American Express, credit cards, many shops also will accept personal checks and, of course, cold cash. Personal checks can come in handy when purchasing a large ticket item requiring shipping. Some shops prefer the personal check to paying commissions on credit cards. A few shops do not accept credit cards at all. If an item needs to be shipped, in the meantime the check can be cleared before the shipment is released.

19. **Beware of international shipping expertise.** Many shops are not used to arranging for international shipping, even though Rio and São Paulo are Brazil's two largest port cities. Shops that often claim to have such expertise actually send an item to a shipper who arranges to air freight the item, which can be very expensive from Brazil. Make sure you clearly understand how the item will be shipped (sea or air freight) and the possible cost. Otherwise, you may be shocked to discover when you return home and receive a fax telling you that your US$5,000 antique furniture purchase will actually cost US$2,500 to ship – by air – and that it's on its way to you collect!

20. **Insist that shops pack your purchases well.** Don't make any assumptions about the packing capabilities of shops, even ones that look like they should know what

they are doing. The concept of "good packing" is by no means universal. What you expect to be good packing may be quite different than what the shop considers to be adequate packing, i.e., item is covered with paper so people on the street won't know what it is! Good packing for us means using lots of bubble wrap, cardboard, and tape if the item is breakable. Not many shops are prepared to do this type of packing. Nonetheless, keep your eye on the packing process and try to get the shop to really do a good job. You may need to hover over them in a back room to ensure that you are getting acceptable packing.

21. **Be prepared to re-pack your purchases.** Try as you may to get a shop to do good packing, many shops lack basic packing tools, supplies, and packing skills – cardboard boxes, cutting knives, tape, and twine or rope. The packing job is often amateurish or just enough to disguise the item with newspaper. Consequently, you may need to re-pack your purchases with the help of hotel personnel or by using your own packing tools and supplies. At a minimum, you should pack strapping tape, address labels, fragile stickers (get these from your airline at check-in time when you leave home – before you need them!), a generous supply of bubble wrap, and twine or rope. A carrying strap often comes in handy for transporting large items.

22. **Expect to encounter some language difficulties when shopping.** Unless you speak Portuguese, shopping without the help of a Portuguese dictionary can be challenging, especially in small shops where no one speaks English. However, personnel in may shops speak some English or they will find someone to help you communicate in their language. You'll seldom be lost for more than five minutes, and sign language and writing notes and drawing pictures will often get the message over. But carrying a small Portuguese/English dictionary is a good idea. It will especially come in handy when it's time to translate a restaurant menu! And it's always a good idea to learn a few Portuguese words to break the ice with locals.

23. **Ask for assistance when necessary.** Although you may encounter language difficulties, the locals often go out of their way to be helpful to visitors. If you get lost or are

having difficulty finding something, don't be shy. Ask for assistance. You may be pleasantly surprised by the helpful response.

24. **Don't expect to find many quality Indian or tribal artifacts.** Much of the quality work sought after by serious collectors has disappeared. Shops specializing in such items tend to offer newly commissioned pieces that are at best good quality handicrafts.

25. **Know your gems and jewelry before you arrive in Brazil.** One of the biggest shopping mistakes many travelers make all over the world is buying gems and jewelry. This is not the time to start getting yourself on the learning curve for gems and jewelry. Often caught up in the herd and the sales psychology of the moment, they lose their good sense by making expensive purchases of things they really don't know much about. Indeed, you can easily pay two to five times more for a similar quality jewelry item than back home, simply because you made an impulsive buy while out shopping with a group of similar impulsive buyers. Whatever you do, learn something about gems and jewelry before you arrive in Brazil. After all, gems and jewelry may be at the very top of your shopping list, whether you realize it or not. It's difficult to avoid such purchases in Brazil which boasts some of the largest selections of gems and jewelry in the world.

26. **Be careful in exchanging your money outside your hotel.** Unlike many other countries, exchanging money at banks in Brazil is inconvenient. It's a waste of time and possibly money. It's much more convenient to exchange some money at your hotel and use credit cards, US dollars, traveler's checks, and personal checks to make purchases.

27. **Check your purchases carefully.** Make sure everything you purchased has been packed and is checked off on your receipt. It's very easy to get distracted and then later find that something got left behind.

28. **Take photos of major purchases.** It's always a good practice to take photos of your purchases for several reasons. First, it's useful to have a visual record of what and where you purchased something. Second, a photo

comes in handy if you're dealing with Customs. Third, should you have a problem with an item being shipped, you can quickly refer to it by the photo. Our recommendation: Take the photo with the merchant who sold it to you. That way you'll know exactly who you dealt with. Better still, the photo will often be a nice memory of the purchased item – and the seller.

29. **Collect business cards.** Whether or not you purchase something from a shop, ask for the business card and write any notes about the shop and potential purchases (item, size, color, price) on the back of the card. If you find something you are interested in but not sure if you want to purchase it before you leave Brazil, ask if you can take a photo and/or if the merchant will write any information on the back of the card about the item. We often find ourselves purchasing items by email or fax once we return home. With information on the business card, as well as a photo, the process of making a long-distance purchase is relatively easy. We no longer say "If only I could remember where I saw that piece" and then regret having left it behind along with appropriate contact information.

30. **Be prepared to hand-carry many purchases.** Some items, such as tribal artifacts and Indian feathered pieces, do not pack and ship well. You may want to pack some of these items in your carry-on luggage or hand-carry them on the plane.

31. **Unlike many other countries, hotels are not major centers for quality shopping.** A few five-star hotels will have two or three good quality shops which primarily offer jewelry, clothing, and handicrafts. The famous jeweler, H. Stern, seems to have a monopoly, with shops in most of Rio's and São Paulo's top hotels. Indeed, their approach seems to be "H. Stern Everywhere" when it comes to the major business and tourist hotels. H. Stern tends to go where the most money is found sleeping and dining.

32. **Shopping malls are not great places for quality shopping.** Shopping malls in Rio and São Paulo are like shopping malls in many other places of the world – decidedly middle-class, mediocre, and crowded with young people, families, and fast food eateries. If you're

interested in a cultural experience, including lots of people watching, these are good places to visit. But when it comes to quality shopping, most shopping malls fall short in the quality department. However, there are always exceptions to this general rule, such as the upscale São Conrado Fashion Mall in Rio. In addition, several top shops often will have branch shops in a few shopping malls simply because that's where the largest volume of people congregate.

33. **Art, antique, and home decorative shops tend to be found together.** Art, antique, and home decorative shoppers will find many of the best shops to be located next to each other along the same street or in the same shopping malls. Indeed, shopping for such items is extremely convenient, and competitive, given the close proximity of similar shops.

34. **Look for websites of shops.** While shops in Brazil have been very slow in using the Internet, more and more shops are doing so, especially in São Paulo. Shops such as René Behar (*www.reneebehar.com.br*) and Ena Beçak (*www.enabecak.com.br*) are using the Internet to communicate with their customers.

35. **Plan to spend Saturdays and Sundays visiting the markets.** Both Rio and São Paulo, as well as nearby towns, have a tradition of weekend markets or fairs that offer a wide variety of arts, crafts, clothes, antiques, and collectibles. Much of the stuff is junk but you may find a few treasures in the midst of the offerings. Many of these places are cultural experiences, good places to rub shoulders with the locals, acquire some unique items at bargain prices, and enjoy the outdoor ambience, complete with music and food.

36. **Check on Saturday shopping hours for shops you plan to visit.** Not all shops are open on Saturday, and many shops close in the early afternoon – around 1pm. To avoid disappointment, check on a shop's hours before planning a Saturday (and definitely Sunday) visit.

37. **Select a hotel near the major shopping areas.** When we travel, we like to have the convenience of a centrally located hotel from which we can go back and forth unloading our loot and relaxing after a hard day of

pounding the pavement. In the case of both Rio and São Paulo, the central shopping area is not the area called Centro – areas that are busy business districts during the day but not much for quality shopping.

38. **Don't expect to get something for nothing.** If a price seems too good to be true, it probably is. Good quality products, especially jewelry, antiques, and art, may not seem cheap in Brazil. But they may be bargains if you compare prices to similar items found in the shops of Paris, London, or New York City.

39. **Use your credit cards whenever possible.** Most shops accept Visa and MasterCard; American Express is less widely accepted. It's always good to charge a purchase just in case you later have a problem with authenticity or shipping. Your credit card company may be able to assist you in resolving such problems. Credit card purchases usually receive the best exchange rates. Be forewarned, a few shops do not accept any credit cards. Those that don't may accept a personal check – even if you take the purchase with you.

40. **Take items with you whenever possible.** While many shops can pack and ship, especially tourist shops selling large and heavy furniture, carpets, and artwork, you may want to take smaller items with you. Don't just take a shop's word that they can ship with no problem. You may discover the cost of shipping a small item can be very expensive, especially when it arrives "collect" by international courier service!

41. **Take your purchases with you as part of your carry-on or check-through luggage.** While shipping from Brazil is relatively easy to arrange, it also can be very expensive. We usually try to take our purchases with us whether they be small or large. In preparation, we usually limit ourselves to one check-through piece of luggage on our flight to Brazil. For the two of us, this allows us three more check-through pieces of luggage on our international flight back home. Our advice: take very little luggage with you on your way to Brazil in anticipation of accumulating purchases along the way that you will want to take with you. Alternatively, if two people are traveling together, take two pieces of luggage and fill the second one primarily with bubble wrap and packing

materials. You still can have two boxes made for larger pieces and bring them home at no additional costs. You'll save a great deal of time and money by planning in this manner. If you purchase an item that can be checked through as luggage, such as a piece of pottery or basket, ask the shop to pack the item well so it can be checked through with your airline as a piece of luggage. Make certain they do pack fragile items well. Be sure to check with your airline on the dimensions of allowable check-through items.

BEWARE OF SCAMS

Although one hopes this will never happen, you may encounter unscrupulous merchants who take advantage of you. Your best line of defense against possible scams is to be very careful wherever you go and whatever you do in relation to handling money. A few simple precautions will help avoid some of these problems:

- **Do not trust anyone with your money** unless you have proper assurances they are giving you exactly what you agreed upon. Trust is something that should be earned – not automatically given to friendly strangers you may like.

- **Do your homework** so you can determine quality and value as well as anticipate certain types of scams.

- **Examine the goods carefully**, assuming something may be or will go wrong.

- **Watch very carefully how the merchant handles items** from the moment they leave your hands until they get wrapped and into a bag.

- **Request receipts** that list specific items and the prices you paid. Although most shops are willing to "give you a receipt" specifying whatever price you want them to write for purposes of deceiving Customs, be careful in doing so. While you may or may not deceive Customs, your custom-designed receipt may become a double-edge sword, especially if you later need a receipt with the real price to claim your goods or a refund. If the shop is to ship, be sure you have a shipping receipt which also specifies insurance against both loss and damage.

- **Take photos of your purchases.** We strongly recommend taking photos of your major purchases, especially anything that is being entrusted to someone else to be packed and shipped. Better still, take a photo of the seller holding the item, just in case you later need to identify the person with whom you dealt. This photo will give you a visual record of your purchase should you later have problems receiving your shipment. You'll also have a photo to show Customs should they have any questions about the contents of your shipment.

- **Protect yourself against scams by using credit cards** for payment, whenever possible – especially for big ticket items which could present problems, even though using them may cost you a little more. Although your credit card company is not obligated to do so, most will ask the merchant for documentation, if you have problems, and if not satisfactorily received, will remove the charge from your bill.

If you are victimized, all is not necessarily lost. You should report the problem immediately to local tourist authorities, the police, your credit card company, or insurance company. While inconvenient and time consuming, nonetheless, in many cases you will eventually get satisfactory results.

SHIP WITH EASE

Shipping can be a problem in Brazil since many shops are not experienced with international shipping. You should not pass up buying lovely items because you feel reluctant to ship them home. Indeed, some travelers only buy items that will fit into their suitcase because they are not sure how to ship larger items. But you can easily ship from Brazil and expect to receive your goods in good condition within a few weeks. We seldom let shipping considerations affect our buying decisions. For us, *shipping is one of those things that must be arranged.* You have numerous shipping alternatives, from hiring a professional shipping company to hand carrying your goods on board the plane. Shipping may or may not be costly, depending on how much you plan to ship and by which means.

Before leaving home, you should identify the best point of entry for goods returning home by air or sea. Once you are in Brazil, you generally have five shipping alternatives:

1. Take everything with you.

2. Do your own packing and shipping through the local post office (for small packages only).

3. Have each shop ship your purchases.

4. Arrange to have one shop consolidate all of your purchases into a single shipment.

5. Hire a local shipper to make all arrangements.

Taking everything with you is fine if you don't have much and if you don't mind absorbing excess baggage charges. If you are within your allowable baggage allowance, you can have large items packed to qualify as part of your luggage. If you have more items than what is allowable, ask about the difference between "Excess Baggage" and "Unaccompanied Baggage." Excess baggage is very expensive, while unaccompanied baggage is less expensive, although by no means cheap.

If items are small enough and we don't mind waiting six to eight weeks, we may send them through the local post office by parcel post; depending on the weight, sometimes air mail is relatively inexpensive through local post offices.

Doing your own packing and shipping may be cheaper, but it is a pain and thus no savings in the long run. You waste valuable time waiting in lines and trying to figure out the local rules and regulations concerning permits, packing, materials, sizes, and weights.

On the other hand, most major shops can ship goods for customers. They often pack the items free and only charge you for the actual postage or freight. If you choose to have a shop ship for you, insist on a receipt specifying they will ship the item. Also, stress the importance of packing the item well to avoid possible damage. If they cannot insure the item against breakage or loss, do not ship through them. Invariably a version of Murphy's Law operates when shipping: *"If it is not insured and has the potential to break or get lost, it will surely break or get lost!"* At this point, seek some alternative means of shipping. If you are shipping only one or two items, it is best to let a reputable shop take care of your shipping.

If you have several large purchases – at least one cubic meter – consider using local shippers since it is cheaper and safer to consolidate many separate purchases into one shipment which is well packed and insured. Sea freight charges are usually figured by volume or the container. There is a minimum charge

– usually you will pay for at least one cubic meter whether you are shipping that much or less. Air freight is calculated using both weight and volume, and usually there is no minimum. You pay only for the actual amount you ship. One normally does not air freight large, heavy items, but for a small light shipment, air freight could actually cost you less and you'll get your items much faster. However, many shops in Rio and São Paulo prefer shipping everything by air freight rather than sea. Since this can be very expensive, make sure you understand the costs before deciding to purchase a large item. When using air freight, use an established and reliable airline. In the case of sea freight, choose a local company which has an excellent reputation among expatriates for shipping goods. Ask your hotel concierge or front desk personnel about reliable shippers. For small shipments, try to have charges computed both ways – for sea and for air freight. Sea shipments incur port charges that can further add to your charges. Port charges at the shipment's point of entry will not normally be included in the price quoted by the local shipping agent. They have no way of knowing what these charges will be. If you have figures for both means of shipping, you can make an informed choice.

We have tried all five shipping alternatives with various results. Indeed, we tend to use these alternatives in combination. For example, we take everything we can with us until we reach the point where the inconvenience and cost of excess baggage requires some other shipping arrangements. We consolidate our shipments with one key shop early in our trip and have shipments from other cities sent to that shop for consolidation.

When you use a shipper, be sure to examine alternative shipping arrangements and prices. The type of delivery you specify at your end can make a significant difference in the overall shipping price. If you don't specify the type of delivery you want, you may be charged the all-inclusive door-to-door rate. For example, if you choose door-to-door delivery with unpacking services, you will pay a premium to have your shipment clear Customs, moved through the port, transported to your door, and unpacked by local movers. On the other hand, it is cheaper for you to designate port to port. When the shipment arrives, you arrange for a broker to clear the shipment through Customs and arrange for transport to your home. You do your own unpacking and dispose of the trash. It will take a little more of your time to make the arrangements and unpack. If you live near a port of entry, you may clear the shipment at Customs and pick up the shipment yourself.

We simply cannot over-stress the importance of finding and

establishing a personal relationship with a good local shipper who will provide you with services which may go beyond your immediate shipping needs. A good local shipping contact will enable you to continue shopping in Brazil even after returning home.

Buying Gems
and Jewelry

A Basic Primer for
Trouble-Free Shopping

OU WALK PAST A SHOP WINDOW FILLED with glittering gems and fabulous looking jewelry. You stop for just a moment – only to look. You're not really planning to buy anything, but the glint of an emerald ring catches your eye. You've heard travelers' tales of the incredible bargains they've gotten in some foreign cities – even saved enough to pay for their trip! Why not just check on the price. Better still, if the shop is offering a free factory tour, perhaps you'll learn something useful about buying Brazilian gems and jewelry. After all, this is the world's largest producer of colored gemstones, especially the popular aquamarine, emerald, and precious topaz – you're at the source which should be much cheaper than elsewhere in the world. And it doesn't cost anything to look! At least not for now.

PUTTING IT ALL IN PERSPECTIVE

Before you become overjoyed with your fortuitous situation, you need to step back a moment to put this all in proper perspective. For every story of an incredible bargain – a traveler who took a chance, made a purchase, and took the gemstone home to find it appraised for 5-10 times what he paid – there is another tale. There are many stories of tourists who took their gemstones home to find the so-called fantastic "ruby" they bought was only a red spinel worth a fraction of what they paid.

In fact, the largest number of tourist complaints lodged with the tourist associations in many of the countries we visit deal with jewelry and gemstone purchases. Many tourists literally get "taken" when they buy jewelry and gems abroad – from fakes and misrepresentation to poor quality stones and jewelry settings. In the end, many of these travelers get much less than what they bargained for – if indeed they bargained at all!

If you will learn about gemstones, realize you can't get something for nothing – anywhere in the world – select the store where you buy using specific criteria, and maintain a healthy level of skepticism, you may be able to make a jewelry purchase you will enjoy for years to come and save money in the process.

❏ The largest number of tourist complaints in many countries we visit deal with jewelry and gemstone purchases.

❏ Smart shoppers learn some basics about gemstones *before* they arrive in Brazil.

❏ A gemstone should have visual beauty, durability, and rarity – well defined concepts in the jewelry business.

❏ Don't confuse karat, which is a measure of gold purity, with carat, which measures the weight of a gemstone.

❏ And don't confuse a so-called Brazilian ruby or rubellite as being a real ruby; it's a red-colored tourmaline.

QUALITIES OF GEMSTONES

A gemstone should have visual beauty, durability, and rarity. **Beauty** is somewhat subjective, with various cultures preferring certain gemstones more than others, and gemstones coming and going in popularity over periods of time. Jade, for example, is generally more highly regarded in Asia than in the rest of the world. Pearls have experienced periods of great popularity only to be held in less regard for periods of time and then to regain popularity again! Beauty may be judged by the depth of color in some stones such as rubies, emeralds and sapphires, or by the absence of color as is the case with most diamonds – though the Argyle diamond mines of Australia provide examples of beautiful champagne, cognac, and pink colors.

Durability refers to three aspects of a gemstone: its hardness, toughness and stability. The hardness of a gemstone is defined by a value on the Mohs hardness scale. A diamond ranks at the very top of the scale – a ten – the hardest gemstone. A diamond is much harder than the next stone on the list – corundum, the mineral of sapphires and rubies, is a nine. The lower the level of hardness, the more easily a stone is scratched. Gemstones with a hardness of less than seven are easily scratched.

Toughness refers to a stone's resistance to cracking, chipping, or breaking. The diamond, by far the hardest stone, lacks toughness. After years of wear, diamonds with exposed edges, for example, those set in Tiffany settings, are likely to have small chipped corners. Obviously a bezel setting that fully encircles the diamond has practical advantages.

Stability refers to a stone's resistance to chemical or structural change. Opals contain water and can lose water in dry air. Now you know why there is often a glass of water in the jeweler's show window. Once water is lost, the opal may crack. Pearls can be damaged by acid, alcohol or perfume. Porous stones, such as turquoise and coral, can pick up oils from the skin or be damaged by harsh cleansing agents.

CONFUSING GEMSTONE NAMES

Most people are familiar with the names of the four precious gemstones: diamond, ruby, sapphire, and emerald. Few people, however, are familiar with the mineral names of precious and semi-precious stones. Sapphire and ruby are the gem names given to the mineral **corundum**. Gem quality corundum which is red is a ruby. Gem quality corundum in any other color is called sapphire. We are most familiar with blue sapphires, but sapphires can be yellow, pink, purple, green, white – even black. By the same token, **beryl** is the mineral name for emeralds and aquamarines. The preeminent beryl is the emerald – a deep green gemstone. The same mineral is called aquamarine in its watery blue shade. Knowing the mineral names for gemstones should help you raise important questions when shopping for gems and jewelry. Such knowledge can save you from making a mistake when buying a gemstone.

Rubies are not mined in South America. While they may be used by local jewelers, they will not be found in abundance since they are imported – primarily from their sources in Burma, northern Thailand, Sri Lanka, and India. However, some jewelers in Brazil may try to sell you a "Brazilian ruby" or rubellite. This is especially likely if you indicate a preference for rubies or want a July birthstone. But if you ask the mineral name of the Brazilian ruby/rubellite, you should be told it is a tourmaline. There is nothing wrong with buying a rubellite. It can be a beautiful stone, but you should know you are getting a tourmaline which is a different mineral than corundum – the mineral of a ruby the world over. Always remember that a Brazilian ruby is not a ruby from Brazil; it is a beautiful red-colored tourmaline and should be priced accordingly.

KARATS AND CARATS

Don't confuse karat, which is a measure of gold purity, with carat, which measures the weight of a gemstone. Most gold jewelry sold in the United States today is either 14 or 18 karat. Once abroad you will find other degrees of purity ranging from 8K in some countries to 22K or higher in much of the Middle East and Asia. In those cultures, where historically much of a family's wealth and certainly a woman's holdings were in jewelry, anything less than 18K gold is not considered as really gold, and 22K and higher is the norm. In much of the world, 14K will be marked as .585 and 18K as .750 which equal the percentages of gold content in the jewelry. In other words, 18K is 75% gold (.750) and 25% base metal. Most gold sold in Brazil is 18K.

Remember that pure gold is soft. To be durable it needs to be alloyed with other more durable metals. A large gold pendant fashioned in 22K gold may be fine, but a ring in 22K will be soft. If the prongs of the setting that hold the gemstone are 22K, you run a high risk of eventually losing the stone. Prongs of no higher than 18K gold are best for setting gemstones. The base metals used as alloys and their amount create the different colors of gold from white gold, to rose gold to yellow gold.

NATURAL STONES, SYNTHETIC STONES, AND SIMULATED GEMS

Natural stones are formed by nature over vast amounts of time and as a result of great amounts of pressure. Natural stones are more scarce and have greater value than synthetic stones. **Synthetic stones** are composed of the exact same substance (chemical properties) as the natural mineral, but have been produced by man in the laboratory. Therefore, it is not easy even for a jeweler to discern the difference between the two since the chemical properties are the same. Because it has been formed by an accident of nature rather than the intent of man, a natural stone usually contains some inclusions. A flawless stone – especially in a mineral that usually contains a variety of inclusions, for example, an emerald – should raise suspicion that the stone may be synthetic. There are sophisticated techniques to differentiate a nearly perfect natural stone from a synthetic, but without the appropriate equipment and training it will be impossible.

A natural stone is worth more than a synthetic; a synthetic stone has more value than a simulated stone. In a **simulated stone**, the optical properties closely resemble the real gem, but the chemical properties are different. The stones look alike to the naked eye, but a jeweler would be able to easily tell the difference. An example is the use of a spinel or a zircon rather than a diamond. Both are real stones, but one has a great deal more value than the others. **Imitation stones** may be made of glass or plastic or they may be composite stones consisting of a thin slice of the gem material under (doublet) or between (triplet) other material of no real value. A synthetic stone can look lovely, but you shouldn't pay a natural gem price for it.

Over the past two decades **"enhancement" of gemstones** has become common. Irradiation may be used to enhance or change the color of many natural stones. Chemical treatment such as bleaching, dyeing, or oiling is used. Heat is used to deepen the color of some gems or improve clarity. These practices are legal but should be disclosed on request. Often they are not disclosed. This isn't necessarily because the salesperson or shop is dishonest; the seller may not know because the individual who supplied the stone to them did not disclose the fact.

THE 4 C'S

Assuming the gem is a natural stone, the color, clarity, cut, and carat weight determine its value. The most valuable **Color** varies with the stone, but generally a stone with uniform and deep saturation of color will have greater value than a light hue or uneven color; however, there is a point at which the stone becomes too dark. It doesn't reflect light and loses sparkle. **Clarity** refers to the absence of inclusions. A flawless stone is one in which no imperfections can be seen at 10X magnification. **Cut** varies with the stone and personal preference. Opaque stones, such as jade, turquoise or coral, are rarely faceted. Since light will not be reflected from within, there is no reason to facet. Instead, they will normally be cut and polished with a rounded top – called **cabachon**. Some transparent stones such as sapphires and rubies can be cut cabachon – especially to show off a star – as well as given faceted cuts. Transparent gemstones are faceted to reflect maximum brilliance. The round brilliant cut, with its modifications – oval, pear, marquise, and heart shapes – and the emerald cut are the most popular today. **Carat** refers to the size of the stone, but size is measured by weight. Two different stones may appear to be different in size because of the way in which they are cut, but in fact be the same weight. Because large stones are rare, one three-carat stone is far more valuable than are three stones of one-carat each – assuming the other three C's are equivalent.

NATURAL PEARLS, CULTURED PEARLS, AND SIMULATED PEARLS

A pearl is formed when a foreign substance finds its way into an oyster – either by an accident of nature or the intention of man. The oyster attempts to protect itself from this foreign substance which may be a grain of sand, a very small pebble or a piece of shell, by secreting successive layers of the same material of which its shell is composed – eventually resulting in a solid mass of a luminous substance which is the pearl. It is perhaps ironic, that the oyster's attempt to protect itself from this small invading body provides the incentive for a much more invasive intrusion on the part of man.

Natural pearls – those formed as a result of an accident of nature – are quite rare. That's due, in part, because it takes yet another accident for them to be found by man. However, **cultured pearls** are formed in exactly the same way by the oyster's secretions. The differences are that man has purposely inserted a small "bead," usually of shell material, into oysters that have been raised for this purpose; they then place the implanted shells in wire baskets and return them to the sea where they are suspended from rafts or buoys. When it is time to harvest the pearls, it isn't hard to find the oysters! Only about 20 percent of the "seeded" oysters will produce quality pearls, but that makes them far less rare than the lucky find of a natural pearl. Few pearls in jewelry stores today are truly natural pearls. Cultured pearls are beautiful and valuable, but should not be confused with a true natural pearl.

Simulated pearls like simulated gemstones have the look of the real thing but have an entirely different composition. Many simulated pearls are pretty plastic!

KNOW WHAT YOU PAY FOR!

So how do you avoid paying natural stone prices for a synthetic or simulated stone? Certainly you should visit one or more of the best jewelry stores in your hometown before you leave home. If you reside in a small town, take the time to visit a large metropolitan area nearby and go to one of the best jewelry stores there. Look at some jewelry – especially the stones you think you may have an interest in acquiring as you travel. Look at the settings and the workmanship of the settings. One of the easiest ways to spot cheap imitation jewelry is not by looking at the stone, but by looking at the workmanship of the setting. The cubic zirconia may fool your untrained eye, but the setting is more likely to give it away!

You might also want to visit a few websites that attempt to educate visitors about gems and jewelry. While these sites are no substitute for actually handling the real thing, they can provide some useful information that may help train your eye and prompt you to ask the right questions when shopping for gems and jewelry. The Better Business Bureau in the United States, for example, offers several useful tips on buying jewelry which are well worth reviewing before you leave for Brazil:

www.bbb.org/library/jewelry.asp

By now it should be obvious that it is difficult for a person untrained in the jewelry trade and without sophisticated equipment at hand to be certain of what he is getting. So what you know about the shop where you make your purchase may be more important than what you know about jewelry.

With this in mind, the following are some guidelines that should help you get a fair deal if you decide to make a jewelry purchase. While you should not fool yourself into believing you are an expert, there is no harm in giving the jeweler the impression you are somewhat gem savvy!

- **Never go to a jewelry store with someone who picked you up on the street!** No matter whether he tells you his uncle owns the store and will give a great deal – just for you, or if he wants to practice his English – avoid him like the tout he is. In the first place, you don't want to make any purchase in any store he would take you to. Quality jewelry stores do not deal in this way. In the second place, you will pay more than you should for any purchase you might make. The tout's commission of anywhere from 10 percent to over 30 percent of your purchase has to come from somewhere!

- **Choose the jewelry store carefully.** If you have a recommendation from a trusted friend – great. If you are staying in a top hotel, ask the concierge for recommendations. They usually know where their satisfied guests shop. Look at jewelry stores in quality shopping areas – the best part of town! The shops within the best hotels, or in the best shopping malls, will most likely have some of the best jewelers. In Rio that means the Copacabana Palace Hotel, Forum de Ipanema, and the São Conrado Fashion Mall. A good hotel or top shopping mall cannot afford to have its reputation tarnished by leasing space to a jeweler who misrepresents his goods. This is no guarantee you may not pay a bit more than you need to if you don't ask for a discount or bargain, but you can feel comfortable that the goods are most likely what they are said to be.

- **Look around at the merchandise in the store.** Does the store sell only jewelry or do they sell souvenirs and other items as well. The best jewelry stores will limit their sales to jewelry and gemstones. The sales staff in a store that only sells jewelry is likely to be far better informed than in the store selling all kinds of merchandise. Although this is generally true, the two biggest purveyors of gemstones and jewelry in Brazil, H. Stern and Amsterdam Sauer, are exceptions. They do sell quality goods and employ a knowledgeable sales staff; however, they also sell a variety of other goods, especially handicrafts, in their larger stones; H. Stern even has its own line of handicraft and folk art stores called Folclore.

- **Do a quick check of the quality of the merchandise you see.** Compare it to the jewelry you saw in the top jewelry store you visited before you left home. Again, remember to look at the settings. Even if you plan to purchase loose stones, look at the gold work on the pieces that are set. It will tell you a great deal about the quality of the shop. If you don't like what you see, move on to another shop.

- **Check whether prices are clearly marked on each item.** What this tells you will vary in different parts of the world. Some places simply don't mark prices on their jewelry, and this is not necessarily a negative about the shop. It may be marked instead with a code that only the jeweler knows. But where prices are clearly marked, you are assured that the price is not set capriciously – even though the amount of the discount may be!

- **Look around at the sales staff.** Do they dress and act professional? Do they seem pushy and try to get people to "buy now" and make a sale, or are they helpful in answering your questions but allow you space to consider your purchase?

- **Look around for the presence of what appear to be gemological instruments.** Are there indications, either by such instruments, or certificates from gemological institutes, that they have accredited gemologists on their staff?

- **Look at any stones through a jewelers' loupe.** Hold the loupe in one hand close to the eye, steadying the hand by resting it against your cheek. With your other hand, bring the stone, held with tweezers, toward the loupe until it is in focus. (You may want to practice holding the stone with tweezers with your jeweler before you leave home!). You should move the stones rather than the loupe.

- **If you expect to make a very expensive purchase, try to deal directly with the manager or owner.** The manager usually knows more about his or her inventory and also may have more flexibility in negotiating a price. Indeed, contacting the manager may result in an additional five to 10 percent discount.

- **If you buy, be sure to get a receipt that is very detailed** as to the gemstone, whether it is a natural stone, the carat weight, the clarity, whether it has been enhanced, and the gold content, if it is a set stone. Be wary of any shop that is hesitant to give you a detailed receipt.

- **Get in writing a guarantee from the shop that you can return the gemstone or jewelry within a reasonable but specific period of time** if you later have it appraised and it turns out not be what it was sold to be. It is also a good idea to be able to return or exchange if you are making an expensive purchase of jewelry for someone who is not with you as you shop.

If you will follow most of the above recommendations, you are likely to get a fair deal on the gem purchases you make. Buy jewelry because you love it – not solely as an investment. It is difficult to know what the market will do, and because of the mark-up on jewelry (unless you truly are buying at wholesale), it will take a long time before you could sell your jewelry (estate) for what you have paid.

Finally, you may choose to make your purchase using your credit card. Although your credit card company is under no obligation to do so, and they do expect that you, the consumer, take reasonable precautions when making purchases, if you do get home to find that your "ruby" is really a red spinel, your credit card company may assist you in getting the seller to take back the stone and refund your money.

Great Destinations

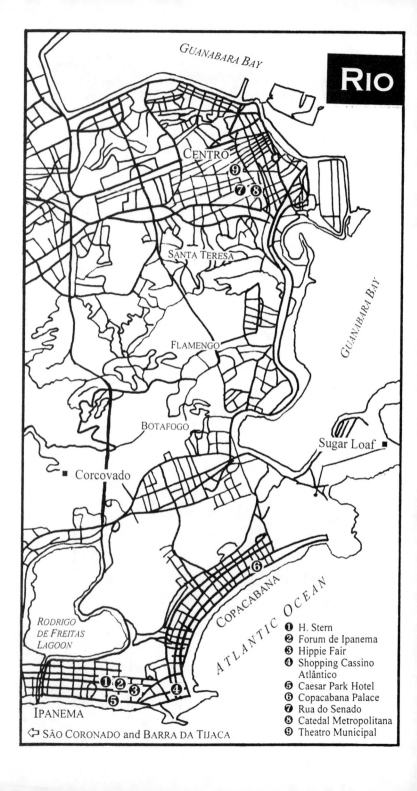

GUANABARA BAY

RIO

CENTRO

❾
❼ ❽

SANTA TERESA

FLAMENGO

GUANABARA BAY

BOTAFOGO

Sugar Loaf ■

■ Corcovado

COPACABANA

❻

ATLANTIC OCEAN

RODRIGO
DE FREITAS
LAGOON

❶ H. Stern
❷ Forum de Ipanema
❸ Hippie Fair
❹ Shopping Cassino
   Atlântico
❺ Caesar Park Hotel
❻ Copacabana Palace
❼ Rua do Senado
❽ Catedal Metropolitana
❾ Theatro Municipal

❶ ❷
❸   ❹
❺

IPANEMA

⇦ SÃO CORONADO and BARRA DA TIJACA

5

Rio de Janeiro

ONLY A FEW CITIES IN THE WORLD CAN CAPture the imagination as much as Rio de Janeiro. An electric city of nearly 10 million people, Rio conjures up some of the best images associated with great travel – beautiful sites, wonderful weather, lush foliage, 23 expansive beaches, friendly people, great shopping, fine cuisine, plenty of outdoor activities, lively entertainment, romantic settings, gorgeous sunsets, and convenient transportation. It's all here in beautiful and seductive Rio. Like Hong Kong or Paris, this is simply a great city, one you won't soon forget. Spend a few days here and you'll quickly get into the fun and sun rhythm that makes Rio such a fabulous place. It's a city that seems to keep on giving the best of the best to both new and seasoned visitors as well as local residents who blend nicely with Rio's year-round vacation and festive culture.

AN ALMOST FORGETTABLE HISTORY

Rio seems obsessed with the present. Energetic and self-possessed, it's becoming more modern as it tears down its old structures in favor of newer buildings. Lacking an illustrious history, the city tends to focus on the present. Originally discovered in 1501 by Portuguese explorers who were lost, the city was founded in 1566. In 1736 it became the colonial capital of Brazil. When Brazil became independent in 1889, Rio continued as the capital of the country and remained so until the capital was moved to the new modernistic interior city of Brasilia in 1960.

Except for a few museums, today's Rio does not dwell on its history nor showcase it well. This is a city of the present – colorful, beautiful, brash, eternal, and very chic. Some observers stretch the imagination by calling this the most beautiful city in the world. Not quite, but close, and by all means extremely picturesque – on par with Hong Kong, Sydney, and Monaco. Hard to explain, Rio is an exciting city that needs to be experienced first-hand.

MEET THE BEAUTIFUL PEOPLE

There's a certain degree of justified narcissism in Rio. Known as the *cariocas*, the locals tend to have a self-possessed and enthusiastic attitude toward their city and life in general. Unlike São Paulo, Rio is not a serious, hard-working city known for its productivity. At least where the tourists and well-heeled gather, down along the beaches, Rio often feels like a big resort where many working locals appear to be on a perpetual beach vacation, socializing and looking for a good time, seven days a week. And they seem to have institutionalized "the good times" with lots of things to do throughout the day and night. Visit Rio and you may quickly succumb to its unique ethos and indulge yourself in its many treasures and pleasures. Don't be surprised to discover you've developed a particular *carioca* attitude toward life without really trying! Two days here and you'll probably become seduced by Rio's good life.

From the moment you arrive until the day you leave, you'll encounter many friendly and easygoing *cariocas* who often refer to themselves as the "beautiful people." Hang around the beaches of Ipanema and Copacabana and you'll see what they mean. There's lots of sexual energy here, from men displaying

❏ Rio is a city of the present – colorful, beautiful, brash, and eternal.

❏ There's a certain degree of narcissism in Rio – locals tend to have a self-possessed and enthusiastic attitude toward their city and life in general.

❏ From the moment you arrive until the day you leave, you'll encounter many friendly and easy going *cariocas* who often refer to themselves as the "beautiful people."

❏ Two or three weeks before Carnival is an excellent time to visit Rio.

well-toned muscles to women presenting lots of cleavage and posterior in public. It's often wall-to-wall beautiful bronze bodies engaged in a huge beachfront social affair played out as beach volleyball, competitive dancing, sunning, swimming, jogging, or just people watching. Many people in nearby bars, cafes, restaurants, and shops also communicate an enthusiastic and passionate attitude which is at times contagious.

But just look around and you'll perhaps understand why this place has an attitude which sometimes borders on the naughty. After all, this is the beautiful beachfront city that has given the world the sensual image of the "girl from Ipanema"; the rhythmic beats of the samba and the bossa-nova; the passions and pleasures of Carnival; the dramatic limestone outcrops and gorgeous city views, vistas, and sunsets from Corcovado and Sugar Loaf; and skimpy fashionable beachwear (string bikinis called *tangas*) and well-toned, tanned, and tantalizing bodies that would be considered a crime to display in some countries.

UNIQUE TREASURES AND PLEASURES

Rio is rich in treasures and pleasures to keep most visitors happily busy, day and night, for at least a week. If you're planning to visit Rio during its four-day Carnival extravaganza, you may want to plan your adventure at least one year in advance since the city is fully booked at that time. In fact, be sure to book your international transportation and Rio accommodations well in advance of the February or March parade dates each year (upcoming Carnival parades take place on February 9-10, 2002, and March 1-2, 2003). If you prefer avoiding this extremely crowded event, mark your calendar accordingly. Two to four weeks before Carnival is an excellent time to visit Rio.

For us, Rio is one of those great destinations that offers a little of everything to everyone, and a lot of many things that make travel such a rewarding experience. An extremely appealing city, Rio can easily be approached from many different "adventure" perspectives: beaches, sports, ecology, architecture, religion, social welfare, dining, entertainment, history, culture, and sightseeing. Best of all, Rio is a great shopping destination offering a wide range of quality local products at very good prices, especially given the favorable exchange rate between the Brazilian *real* (R$) and the US dollar (US$). As we went to press in early 2001, the exchange rate stood at nearly two *reais* to the U.S. dollar (R$2.13 = US$1). The devaluation of the *real* in 1999 nearly doubled the value of the US dollar in Brazil. You can easily spend a week in Rio going treasure hunting through its many neighborhoods, shopping malls, street shops, and markets for everything from art and antiques to clothes and jewelry. Like so many other things in Rio, shopping is great fun and it puts you in contact with many "beautiful people" who seem to have a contagious passion for life!

GETTING TO KNOW YOU

As soon as you arrive in Rio, you'll find the place visually appealing – except for lots of disfiguring graffiti – with its expansive beaches stretching from the southeast to the south and with lush rainforests, hills, and mountains lying to the west. The famous limestone outcrops, Corcovado and Pão de Açucar (Sugar Loaf), lie immediately to the west and east of Botafogo, which is just north of the southeastern beach area of Copacabana. Most visitors prefer staying in the south (Zona Sul) near the popular beaches, especially around Copacabana and Ipanema, where most of the dining, shopping, and entertainment action can be found.

❏ Shopping is great fun and it puts you in contact with many of Rio's "beautiful people."

❏ Rio is a relatively easy city to get around in once you get an initial orientation and learn to use taxis and the subway.

❏ Centro is where you will find much of Rio's history and culture. Its narrow streets, wonderful colonial architecture, small bars and restaurants, and delightful tram make this one of the city's most interesting areas.

❏ Zona Sul (South) is Rio's popular tourist destination – the area that gives Rio its image as a fun, festive, and sensual beachfront city.

In preparation for Rio, you may want to explore a few key websites that focus on Rio. Three of our favorite sites include:

www.ipanema.com
www.destinationrio.com
www.rio.rj.gov.br/riotur

These sites provide lots of useful information on Rio, including insights on tours, dining, accommodations, sightseeing, museums, sporting events, nightlife, and Carnival. The Ipanema site (also found at *www.riodejaneiroguide.com*) includes a wealth of information on the city – by far the best city website in Brazil. The other two Rio sites are sponsored by the city's tourism authority, RIOTUR (see page 113), and are also loaded with useful travel information. Once you arrive in Rio, be sure to pick up a good map of the city. *The Guide to Rio* is one of the most useful map/guidebook combinations (in both English and Spanish) which is available at most bookstores. You'll also find a few other English language guidebooks which may be available free of charge from your hotel concierge – *Rio de Janeiro Guide: Concierge* and *Rio This Month*. Armed with a good map and guidebooks, as well as a handy compass, you should be well prepared to tackle this city with relative ease.

Rio is a relatively easy city to get around in once you get an initial orientation and learn to use taxis and the subway. While the city is divided into several districts, most people orient themselves to three major areas: north (Zona Norte), central (Centro), and south (Zona Sul). The international airport is located in the north. The south is the most popular destination for visitors. However, the central area, which is Rio's business and residential area, is well worth spending a day or two exploring its many museums, churches, shops, narrow streets, and old neighborhoods.

CENTRO

If you only visit Rio for its southern beaches, restaurants, and entertainment, you're likely to miss some of the city's most interesting places which tend to be concentrated in the central area. This is Rio's central business and residential district which stretches from the domestic airport (Santos Dumont) in the east to Fatima and St. Teresa districts in the southwest. Known as the city's older section, Centro consists of numerous office buildings, commercial establishments, small businesses, shops, restaurants, bars, churches, museums, and theaters. While this area may initially look intimidating because of its complexity and congestion, with a decent map and compass, you'll be able to easily navigate the area. Centro is where you will find much of Rio's history and culture. Its narrow streets, wonderful colonial architecture, small bars and restaurants, and delightful tram ride into hilly Santa Teresa District make this one of the most interesting areas of Rio which is often overlooked by many visitors who confine their "Rio experience" to the beaches, restaurants, shops, and sightseeing in the south. Centro exudes a great deal of history, culture, and local character. Here's where you encounter delightful old Rio, which contrasts greatly with the heavily touristed new Rio in the south. You can easily and inexpensively reach this area by taking the subway from the Copacabana area (the station is just three blocks north of the Copacabana Palace Hotel and the fast ride only costs R$1).

While Centro lacks the beaches and festive air of south Rio, it offers many historical, cultural, and architectural pleasures and shopping treasures. Some of the major highlights of Centro include the Carioca Aqueduct (Aqueduto da Carioca) where you can catch the delightful tram; National Library (Biblioteca Nacional); São Sebastião Cathedral (the beehive Catedral de São Sebastião do Rio de Janeiro); National Museum of Fine Arts (Museu Nacional de Belas Artes); Municipal Theater (Teatro Municipal); National History Museum (Musu Histórico Nacional); Museum of the Small Farm of the Sky (Museu Chácara do Céu); Convent of St. Anthony (Convento do Santo Antônio); Palio Tradentes; da Ordem Terceira do Monte do Carmo; and Paço Imperial. While the main street in this area, Avenue Rio Branco, has numerous small shops, the most interesting shopping area is found in the many antique and furniture shops along Rue du Senado and Rue du Lavradio (near São Sebastião Cathedral). This area has many interesting small restaurants as well as the famous old grand Colombo café and restaurant with its beautiful stained glass windows and old world atmosphere – a "must visit" for lunch when in the Avenue Rio Branco area.

Whatever you do, make a special effort to visit Centro during your stay in Rio. Treat yourself to lunch at Colombo, enjoy a tram ride, and explore the area's many museums, churches, and shops as well as enjoy the delightful architecture and ambience of narrow streets, alleys, and residential sections, especially near the Museu Chácara do Céu. You can easily spend a full day in Centro enjoying its many sites, shops, and restaurants. Full of character, this area won't disappoint you. It may well become the highlight of your visit to Rio!

ZONA SUL (SOUTH)

The southern section is Rio's popular tourist destination. While often noisy and congested, it's what gives Rio its image as a fun, festive, and sensual beachfront city. Miles of expansive beaches with backdrops of gorgeous tropical mountains make this area visually stunning. Here's where tourists indulge themselves in Rio's many popular treasures and pleasures. Indeed, this is the area that yields popular images of both Rio and Brazil – the two famous outcrop mountains (Corcovado and Pão de Açucar) for sightseers, the beaches of Copacabana and Ipanema, and many famous hotels, restaurants, bars, cafes, and shops. This area, in effect, is Rio's big playground for experiencing the city's many sun and surf pleasures. The Ipanema area is also Rio's most fashionable shopping area.

Zona Sul is generally divided into five major sections that spread along the beach, beginning with Copacabana in the southeast and ending with Barra da Tijuca in the southwest:

Copacabana, Ipanema, Leblon, São Conrado, and Barra da Tijuca. Each area has its own particular appeal to visitors.

COPACABANA

Copacabana is everyone's favorite destination, a "must visit" area of Rio. This picture postcard area, with its wide curving beach, is where much of the beach action is found. Indeed, looking at, or being on, the beach seems to be everyone's favorite activity in Copacabana, including many beach bums who seem to make life on Copacabana a career. A great place for photo opportunities, this is a major center for the beautiful and energetic people engaged in a variety of beachfront activities, from sun worshiping, swimming, and volleyball to kite flying, musical performances, schmoozing, and drinking. Outdoor cafes, bars, restaurants, hotels, shopping, entertainment, beachfront juice kiosks, and hawkers give this area a truly festive character. Rio's best and most famous grand hotel is located here, the Copacabana Palace, along with several other top properties: Le Meridien, Rio Atlântica, Rio Othon Palace, Sofitel Rio Palace, and the new Marriott Rio. The nearly three kilometer road, Avenue Atlântica, as well as a parallel sidewalk for strollers and joggers, rings one of Rio's most beautiful and popular stretches of beach. You can easily wile away the day just walking up and down the beachfront, occasionally stopping for drinks, food, or shopping. Better still, stay at the grand dame of Brazilian hotels, the Copacabana Palace, and indulge your travel fancies. Copacabana may quickly seduce you.

IPANEMA

Located immediately south of Copacabana, beginning at Forte de Copacabana or Arpoador Beach, and stretching nearly three kilometers west, is another one of Rio's expansive beach areas that competes well with Copacabana for beach crowds and leisure activities. But this area has more class and is much more romantic than Copacabana. Chic, sophisticated, and laid back, it's where the money, both old and new, resides. A more elegant area than Copacabana, Ipanema is where you will find most of Rio's fashionable shopping – top jewelry stores and boutiques – which tends to be concentrated along the area's main street, Rua Visconde de Perajá, located two blocks inland and parallel to the beach, and Rua Garcia d'Avila. The beachfront road, Avenue Francisco Otaviano, includes one of Rio's top hotels, the Caesar Park, as well as several other hotels, restaurants, and outdoor cafes. Many visitors prefer staying in the Ipanema area because it's quieter and less hectic than more exuberant Copacabana.

LEBLON

Leblon is basically the western extension of Ipanema, a bridge between Ipanema and São Conrado. The beach here is only appropriate for sunbathing since the waters are often polluted. Leblon includes a few excellent restaurants and interesting shops. It's not a major destination for most visitors but it can offer a few surprises.

SÃO CONRADO

This is a very quiet area located directly west of Ipanema and Leblon. Except for those staying at the Hotel Intercontinental and Hotel Sheraton, few visitors get to nearby São Conrado. That's unfortunate since this area has one of Rio's most beautiful and uncrowded beaches. The area is visually spectacular with a gorgeous mountain backdrop from which parasailers and hang-gliders regularly circle the area like graceful birds. São Conrado also boasts one of Rio's best upscale shopping centers, the São Conrado Fashion Mall, which is located just behind the Hotel Intercontinental. If you want to avoid the crowds and noise of Copacabana and Ipanema, this is a delightful place to stay.

BARRA DA TIJUCA

Located further west of São Conrado, Barra da Tijuca is Rio's major middle-class suburban residential and commercial area. While not many visitors venture this far west, dedicated shoppers discover Rio's largest complex of shopping malls and shopping centers here. Barra da Tijuca also boasts some of Rio's best beaches and restaurants. Indeed, Rio's longest stretch of beach – 18 kilometers in length – is found here. It's especially popular on weekends with Rio's suburban residents.

LARANJEIRAS, FLAMENGO, BOTAFOGO, CORCOVADO, AND PÃO DE AÇUCAR

Forming a transition area between Centro and Zona Sul, this area is home to two of Rio's major sightseeing attractions – the stunning mountain outcrops of Corcovado and Pão de Açucar. Encompassing Guanabara Bay, this area also includes two popular beaches for sunbathing – Flamengo and Botafogo. Since the waters here are polluted, Flamego and Botafogo beaches are not appropriate for swimming. Viewed from the peaks of Corcovado and Pão de Açucar, this is visually one of the most attractive areas in Rio – truly a photographer's paradise. Whatever you do, make sure you play tourist for a day by visiting both Corcovado and Pão de Açucar. They will not disappoint you. This area also boasts a few excellent arts and crafts shops, especially in Laranjeiras and Botafogo districts.

THE STREETS OF RIO

Getting around Rio is relatively easy, although not always safe. Rio has its share of pickpockets and other criminals that occasionally prey on tourists. However, during the past two years local officials have made concerted efforts to lower Rio's crime rate, especially in the tourist areas. Nonetheless, you should be careful when it comes to securing valuables and visiting various areas of the city.

The best ways to get around Rio are by foot, taxi, subway, and tram. Many locals use buses, but they are not easy to use and safety (pickpockets and thieves) is a major issue. While you can rent a car, doing so is both expensive and inconvenient given traffic and parking problems. Yellow taxis with blue stripes are easy to find and relatively inexpensive. Their flag initially drops at R$2. Most short rides, between Copacabana and Ipanema, for example, will cost under R$5. Longer trips from Copacabana to the central business district will cost about R$15. Trips to the international airport will cost about R$30.

❑ Copacabana is everyone's favorite destination – a major center for Rio's beautiful and energetic people engaged in a variety of beachfront activities.

❑ Chic, sophisticated, and laid back, Ipanema is where the money, both old and new, resides. It's where you will find most of Rio's fashionable shopping.

❑ Yellow taxis with blue stripes are easy to find and relatively inexpensive.

❑ Rio's subway is very convenient and inexpensive.

❑ The tram in Centro and Santa Teresa is one of the most enjoyable rides in Rio.

Rio's subway is very convenient and inexpensive. It operates from 5am to 11pm, except on Sunday. While its coverage of the city is limited for local residents (south to north and north to west), it does connect Copacabana to Centro, a major connection for visitors who stay in the Ipanema and Copacabana area and who wish to visit the Centro area. If you're traveling from Copacabana to Centro, use the subway. It's both fast and inexpensive with eight stops along the way. Most rides cost R$1.

The tram or street car is one of the most enjoyable rides in Rio. It takes you up and down some of the city's steepest and most interesting streets. The major line originates at the city's old aqueduct (Aqueduto da Carioca), which is located adjacent to the conical Catedral Metropolitana in Centro. Costing only R$.60, the charming tram takes you up and down hills, past bars and restaurants, and through quaint neighbors of Santa Teresa District. It's a great way to see another interesting area of the city that is often overlooked by visitors.

SHOPPING RIO

One of the real highlights of visiting Rio is shopping. It's both educational and fun, a great way to learn about local products and meet many interesting people. While Rio is by no means a shopper's paradise on the par with Paris, London, New York, Singapore, or Hong Kong, it does hold its own in the shopping department. This is especially true when it comes to finding unique gems and jewelry, enjoying the ambience of weekend flea markets, rummaging for antiques and collectibles, and discovering lovely handcrafted items. Given today's favorable exchange rates with the US dollar, visitors from the United States increasingly find good buys in Rio.

Given Rio's many colorful weekend markets, both indoor and outdoor, many visitors plan to spend part of Saturday and Sunday leisurely visiting the markets. Indeed, you can easily spend your weekend just shopping in these places where you are likely to discover many interesting handicrafts, clothes, accessories, art, antiques, and collectibles. During the week you may want to concentrate on Rio's many shopping centers and shops that line its major shopping areas.

Most small shops are open Monday through Friday from 9am to 6pm and on Saturday from 9am to 1pm or 2pm. Most large shopping centers and malls are open Monday through Friday from 10am to 10pm and on Saturday from 10am to 8pm; some of these places also stay open on Sunday. Hours of weekend markets vary, depending on the particular market. Some are only open on Saturday whereas others are open on Sunday. And some are open from 8am to 1pm and others from 9am to 6pm. Before planning to shop markets on Saturday or Sunday, be sure to check the opening times and hours for different markets.

Prices in most shops are fixed. However, expect to bargain

in shops selling high-ticket items, such as gems, jewelry, and antiques, as well as in weekend markets. Discounts can range from 5 percent to 50 percent, depending on the merchant and your bargaining skills.

WHAT TO BUY

Shops and markets in Rio offer a wide range of products for shoppers. You'll find everything from top quality gems, jewelry, art, antiques, clothes, accessories, and handicrafts to inexpensive beachwear and souvenirs. From the sophisticated to the trendy, there's something for everyone in Rio. You will most likely find the following products in the various shops and markets of Rio:

❑ **Gemstones and jewelry:** While you'll find several jewelry shops in Rio offering a wide range of gemstones and fashionable jewelry, including many unique gold designs, Rio's two most famous integrated jewelers are **H. Stern** (Tel. 259-7442) and **Amsterdam Sauer** (Tel. 512-9878). As vertically integrated jewelers, they mine, cut, and polish gems as well as design and produce fashionable jewelry. They also function as wholesale dealers to gem and jewelry buyers throughout the world. Located next to each other on Rua Visconde de Pirajá (Nos. 490 and 484) in Ipanema, these jewelers also have several branch shops in Rio. Their two main shops also function as museums and demonstration centers for tour groups, especially for cruise ship passengers who make the obligatory visit to these two large showrooms. Other gem and jewelry shops are found in several upscale hotels and in numerous shopping centers in Ipanema (Forum de Ipanema), Leblon (Shopping Da Gávea), Copacabana (Shopping Cassino Atlântico), and São Conrado (Fashion Mall). We especially like **Akbar** (Tel. 522-3300), a small but top quality shop, in Shopping Cassino Atlântico.

> ❑ Shopping is one of Rio's real highlights – finding unique gems and jewelry, enjoying the ambience of weekend flea markets, rummaging for antiques and collectibles, and discovering lovely hand crafted items.
>
> ❑ Most small shops are open Monday through Friday from 9am to 6pm and on Saturday from 9am to 1pm or 2pm.
>
> ❑ Most shops have fixed prices. Expect to bargain in shops selling high-ticket items, such as gems, jewelry, and antiques, as well as in weekend markets.
>
> ❑ Brazil is the world's largest producer of colored gemstones and gold.

You'll also find lots of interesting fashion and craft jewelry offered in several nice shops in Ipanema (Forum de Ipanema) and São Conrado (Fashion Mall) and in the various weekend markets, especially at the weekly Hippie Fair (Feira Hippie) in Copacabana and the biweekly market at the Brazilian Jockey Club in Gávea (Babilônia Feira Hype). We especially like the fashion jewelry available at **Francesca Romana** and unique gold jewelry at **Lisht** (both found at São Conrado Fashion Mall and Forum de Ipanema).

❑ **Art:** The art scene in Rio is very colorful and lively. Many of the weekend markets include relatively inexpensive paintings that make memorable souvenirs of Rio; the most extensive such offerings are found in the outdoor Sunday **Hippie Fair** in Ipanema. Serious collectors of quality paintings should visit several art galleries on the lower floor of **Shopping Cassino Atlântico**, which is attached to the Sofitel Rio Palace Hotel at the southern end of Copacabana; **Rio Design Center** in Leblon; and **Shopping Center da Gávea** in Gávea. You'll also find art and art books for sale at the Museum Shop of the National Art Museum (Museu Nacional de Balas Artes) in Centro.

A few shops also carry a nice range of Brazilian folk art which is often found in shops that offer handicrafts. One of the best folk art galleries is **Pé de Boi** (Rua Ipiranga, 55, Laranjeiras, Tel. 285-4395, *www.pedeboi.com.br*) which is located between Botafogo and Centro, just west of Flamengo. Some of the best art from the Brazilian Indian tribes is found at **Brumado** (Rue Das Laranjeiras 486, Loja B, Laranjeiras, Tel. 558-2275) and **Artindia**, the small art shop attached to the Indian Museum (Museu do Índio, Rua das Palmeiras 55, Botafogo, Tel. 286-2097).

For current art exhibits, contact your hotel concierge or check the local newspapers and the *Vejo Rio* magazine.

❑ **Antiques:** Rio has numerous antique shops and markets that can easily keep you busy "antiquing" the city for three or more days. The antiques range from old colonial furniture, glassware, and porcelain to silver, paintings, jewelry, and many small collectibles. Rio's antique centers are very well defined – shopping centers primarily devoted to art, antiques, and collectibles. South Rio has the largest concentration of such centers: **Rua Siqueira Campos**, **Shopping Cassino Atlântico**, and **Rio Design Center**. On weekends, both Shopping Cassino Atlântico (Saturday) and Rio Design

Center (Sunday) become antique markets with dealers setting up small stalls along the hallways to sell their wares.

The Centro area has one major antique and furniture area that is well worth exploring. If you're interested in antiques, head for the intersection of **Senado and Lavradio** streets (Rua do Senado and Rua do Lavradio) which is near the Catedral Metropolitana. Running south and west, these two streets are lined with numerous antique and furniture shops. You can easily spend three to four hours browsing the many interesting shops along these streets. Catering primarily to local residents and expatriates, the shops here offer many unique products at relatively good prices. Many of the shops primarily specialize in furniture, lamps, ceramics, and small collectibles. On the first Saturday of each month, Lavradio Street, which has recently undergone a major facelift (the facades of the old buildings are designated a UNESCO Heritage area), becomes a festive street market.

❑ **Clothes:** Rio is especially noted for its casual fashions, sportswear, T-shirts, and children's clothes. You'll find both imported and local brands in Rio's many department stores and shopping centers. For a good range of clothes, be sure to visit Mesbla Department Store in Centro (Rua do Passeio 42/56), Rio Sul Shopping Center, Forum de Ipanema, and São Conrado Fashion Mall. Many shops in Ipanema and Copacabana sell Rio's signature swimwear, the skimpy string bikini called *tangas.* T-shirts abound in shops, markets, and sightseeing centers.

❑ **Accessories:** From jewelry and belts to handbags and shoes, Rio's fashion malls and shops are well stocked with the latest in accessories. For everyday fashion jewelry at excellent prices, be sure to visit the ever popular **Francesca Romana** at the São Conrado Fashion Mall (Tel. 322-2197) and Forum de Ipanema (521-0877). For uniquely designed one-of-a-kind small handbags that approximate a work of art, be sure to visit **Glorinha Paranaguá**, a charming little (tiny) shop located near the Forum de Ipanema (Rua Visconde de Pirajá, 365, Tel. 267-4295). Other shops in and around Forum de Ipanema are well stocked with fashion accessories.

❑ **Leather:** Fashionable leather goods, from shoes, handbags, and belts to luggage, jackets, and wallets, are favorite buys for many visitors. We especially like the attractive leather handbags available at the **Victor Hugo** shops which are found in several locations in the city (Rua Visconde de Pirajá,

507, in Ipanema, Tel. 259-9699, plus six other locations). **Santa Marinella** at Barrashopping (Tel. 431-9829) and Shopping Center Rio Sul (Tel. 275-9346) also has very fashionable leather handbags. **Swains** at Rio Sul (Tel. 541-0606) and São Conrado Fashion Mall (Tel. 322-0757) offers a nice selection of leather shoes, handbags, and belts. Several vendors at the weekend Hippie Fair offer a wide selection of inexpensive leather goods.

❑ **Handicrafts:** You'll find good quality handicrafts in Rio along with some tourist kitsch. One of the best handicraft shops is actually operated by the gemstone and jewelry giant, H. Stern – **Folclore** (Hotel Inter-Continental, Tel. 322-1831 and in the main H. Stern shop at Rua Visconde de Pirajá, 490 (Tel. 259-7442) in Ipanema. A few shops also offer good quality folk handicrafts and arts and crafts from various Indian tribes. We especially like **Pé de Boi** (Rua Ipiranga, 55, Laranjeiras, Tel. 285-4395, *www.pedeboi.com.br*) for its local arts and crafts. For Indian arts and crafts, be sure to visit **Brumado** (Rue das Laranjeiras 486, Loja B, Laranjeiras, Tel. 558-2275) and **Artindia**, the small art shop attached to the Indian Museum (Museu do Índio, Rua das Palmeiras, 55, Botafogo, Tel. 286-2097).

Rio's numerous weekend markets are well stocked with locally-produced handicrafts. The famous **Hippie Fair** in Ipanema (Sunday, 9am to 6pm) includes numerous arts and crafts stalls offering everything from craft jewelry and stuffed toys to leather goods and paintings. The biweekly market at the Brazilian Jockey Club (Babilônia Feira Hype) offers a wide range of handcrafted items.

❑ **Gifts and souvenirs:** While the weekend markets, museum shops, and the shops near the major sightseeing attractions (Corcovado and Pão de Açucar) are good places to find unique gift and souvenir items, you'll also discover quality gift items at **H. Stern Home** (Rua Garcia D'Ávila, 102/108, Tel. 239-7845) in Ipanema as well as **Sobotka & Co.** (Tel. 422-0972)at the São Conrado Fashion Mall.

❑ **Music:** Rio has its own beat which is associated with many different music venues. Brazilian music includes MPB (Música Popular Brasileira), samba-canção, bossa-nova, chorinho, pagode, tropicalistes, jazz, Afro-beat, and other combinations. If you get into Brazilian music, you'll probably want to purchase CDs. You'll find several music shops that offer an excellent range of music: **Collector's** (Rua Visconde de Pirajá, Tel. 239-6793), **Gabriela** (Shopping Center Gávea, Rua Marquês de São Vicente, 52, Loja 138/139, Tel. 374-3245), and **Gramophone** (Shopping Center Gávea, Loja 107, Tel. 274-2495).

WHERE TO SHOP

The largest concentration of shopping of interest to visitors is found in South Rio, especially in the major shopping centers and weekend markets, and in a few shops between South Rio and Centro. While Centro has some department stores and shops, aside from the antique and second hand district (Senado and Lavradio streets), there is not a great deal of interesting shopping found in Centro. Most visitors go to Centro for sightseeing and culture.

Shopping centers in Rio come in many different forms. Huge shopping complexes such as Barrashopping and Rio Sul, which include hundreds of shops and large food courts, are similar to shopping malls found in North America; they are especially popular with local residents who visit these places with their families. Other shopping centers, such as Forum de Ipanema, Rua Siqueira Campos, Shopping Cassino Atlântico, and Rio Design Center, are older and much smaller; they tend to specialize in particular product lines, such as jewelry, fashion, art, antiques, and home decorative items.

SOUTH RIO

Most shopping in South Rio is concentrated in a few shopping centers in Copacabana, Ipanema, Leblon, Gávea, and São Conrado as well as along a few major shopping streets, such as Rua Visconde de Pirajá in Ipanema. Farther west of São Conrado is Barra da Tijuca with its own style of suburban shopping.

SHOPPING CENTERS

❏ **São Conrado Fashion Mall:** *Open Monday through Thursday, 10am to 9pm; Friday and Saturday, 10am to 11pm; and Sunday, 3pm to 9pm.* Located near the Intercontinental Hotel in São Conrado, this is Rio's most fashionable shopping mall. Filled with over 100 upscale shops and restaurants, the Fashion Mall has great ambience as far as Rio's shopping centers go. This shopping center is filled with fashion boutiques, leather stores, and jewelry shops Some of the shops are branches of stores found at other shopping centers in Rio. Look at

Manufact and Swains (Tel. 322-0757) for good quality handbags, shoes, and belts; Francesca Romana (Tel. 322-2197), Lisht (Tel. 322-5779), and Augusto for fashionable and quality jewelry; and Golden Gate (Tel. 322-4779) for international home decorative items. For restaurants with generous proportions, try Alvaro's Bar (Brazilian) and Enotria (Italian).

❑ Forum de Ipanema: *Open Monday through Friday, 10am to 7pm, and Saturday, 10am to 2pm.* Located in the heart of Ipanema's central shopping district, along Rua Visconde de Pirajá and next to the Varig Airlines office, this two-story older shopping center includes many fashion boutiques and designer jewelry shops. On the ground floor, Mémories (#107, Tel. 267-2495) offers an excellent selection of antiques and collectibles; Lisht (Tel. 522-8618) displays some beautiful jewelry in its signature gold and diamond designs, although the selections appear better at its more attractive São Conrado Fashion Mall shop; and Sabbá (Tel. 247-4788), Carla Amorium (Tel. 322-6533), and Wolfgang Badofszky offer many unique and attractively designed jewelry pieces. On the upper floor, Francesca Romana (Tel. 521-0877), with its reasonably priced David Yurman-style jewelry, offers very fashionable neck pieces and rings – one of Rio's most popular fashion jewelry shops. Nearby is Alberto Sabina with interesting costume jewelry and Tereza Xavier (Tel. 523-6552) with nicely designed jewelry, shoes, and sunglasses.

❑ Rua Siqueira Campos: *Open Monday through Friday, 10am to 6pm, and Saturday, 10am to 1pm.* Located in the heart of Copacabana at Rua Siqueira Campus, 143, this is Rio's best art, antique, and home decorative center with nearly 100 shops offering antiques, collectibles, objets d'art, chandeliers, paintings, and carpets. Its two floors are jam-packed with quality shops of special interest to collectors and home decorators. If you're looking for antique religious figures, this is the place to visit. Some of best shops here include Arte & Antiguidade (Tel. 235-0935) with its furniture, porcelain, paintings, chandeliers, rugs, silver, and religious altars; Mury & Saad (Tel. 549-8165) for quality furniture, pedestals, chandeliers, lamps, and paintings; Machado Antiguidades (Tel. 521-0030) for numerous religious figures and top quality antiques and collectibles; and Equinocial Antiqui-dades (Tel. 548-9570) for nautical items such as old sextons, telescopes, pots, and model ships. Other exceptionally attractive art and antique shops include **Quadros** (Tel. 256-2759), **Fernando Braga** (Tel. 548-5393), **Sales & Fischer** (Tel. 236-3345), **Mariu's Antiquários** (Tel. 235-0049), **Antonio Caetano** (Tel. 245-4408), **Herbert Antiguidades** (Tel. 255-3433), and **Kiko** (Tel. 256-8711).

❑ **Shopping Cassino Atlântico:** *Open Monday through Friday, 9am to 9pm, and Saturday, 11am to 7pm.* Located at the southern tip of Copacabana and attached to the Hotel Sofitel Rio Palace, this is one of Rio's major centers for art, antiques, collectibles, jewelry, and home decorative items. Its densely occupied four floors, connected by elevators and escalators, are filled with interesting shops offering a wide range of products. While primarily an antique center, you'll also find several shops offering good quality jewelry, home decorative items, and paintings. One of Brazil's best art dealers is found here, **Dag Saboya** (Tel. 287-1456), although the shop itself is not very impressive. Another excellent art gallery is **Mauricio Pontual** (Tel. 522-5810), which has several oils and prints on display. For good quality antiques, collectibles, and home decorative items, be sure to visit these excellent shops: **Belle des Belles** (Tel. 267-8246), **Rue Jadis** (Tel. 522-3873), **R & W Antiguidades** (Tel. 521-5598), **Carthago** (Tel. 522-0125), **Memories** (Tel. 247-5324), **Pôrto Velho** (Tel. 522-4978), **g. lamego** (Tel. 267-7725), and **Villa B Orient** (Tel. 513-4256). For a unique collection of tribal handicrafts, visit **Ivotici**. On the lower level, look for a very small shop that deals in gems – **Crystal Shine** (Tel. 287-9466). For good quality jewelry, visit **H. Stern, Freddy's, Dischon,** and **Samy's.** Our favorite gem and jewelry shop here is **Akbar** (Tel. 522-3300), a small but very exclusive shop which also will custom design as well as copy jewelry within 48 hours. On Saturday vendors turn Shopping Cassino Atlântico into a flea market as they set up stalls in the hallways to sell all kinds of antiques and collectibles.

❑ **Rio Design Center:** *Open Monday through Saturday, 10am to 10pm, and Sunday, noon to 10pm.* Located at Rua Ataulfo de Paiva, 280 in Leblon, this four-story shopping center includes several upscale home decorative shops offering everything from furniture and rugs to lamps and fabrics. **Orient Express** (Tel. 274-2545) offers a good selection of imported oriental rugs. On Sunday this shopping center is transformed into a flea market as vendors set up stalls in the hallways to sell antiques and collectibles. If you visit the Saturday flea market at Shopping Cassino , you'll notice many of the same vendors are doing business at the Rio Design Center on Sunday. Indeed, if you've shopped at Shopping Cassino Atlântico on Saturday, there may be no need to visit here on Sunday.

❑ **Shopping Center da Gávea:** Located along Rua Marquês de São Vicente in Gávea (northwest of Leblon), this older and somewhat worn shopping center includes over 200 shops: several excellent art galleries, furniture stores, antique and home decorative shops, jewelers, and children's shops. Most of the art galleries, antique dealers, and home decorative shops are located on the second floor. Some of the most interesting shops here include **Sartun** for antiques, silver, and furniture; **Joachim Mitnitzky** for very expensive antiquities, furniture, ceramics, and paintings; **Contorno** for paintings; **Bronze** for bronze sculptures and paintings; **Rosa Kochen** for decorative bowls, plates, and lamps from Brazil, Italy, and Morocco; **Amniemeyer** for contemporary paintings and sculptures; **Galeria G** for good quality Brazilian paintings and sculptures; and **GC Galeria Chagall** for paintings. For music, look for **Gramophone**.

❑ **Rio Sul Shopping Center:** *Open Monday to Friday, 10am to 10pm, and Sunday, 3pm to 9pm.* Located at Avenida Lauro Müller, 116 in Botafogo. This popular shopping center has nearly 450 retail shops, including a large food court. One of Rio's first large shopping centers. Primarily appeals to locals with its many boutiques and food outlets.

❑ **Barrashopping:** *Open Monday through Saturday, 10am to 10pm, and Sunday, 3pm to 9pm.* Located five kilometers west of São Conrado at Barra da Tijuca, this is Latin America's largest shopping complex with over 500 shops. Especially popular with local suburban residents, this can be an overwhelming shopping complex for first-time visitors. Noted for its huge Statue of Liberty at the main entrance and a monorail (R$2) that links various sections of the shopping complex, Barrashopping seems to have everything you ever wanted in a shopping center – trendy shops, entertainment, restaurants, food court, and supermarket with wonderful fruits, vegetables, and a deli. You can easily spend hours here roaming the hallways and riding the monorail. Many shops, such as **H. Stern, Lisht, Manufact, Ganish,** and **Santa Marinella,** are branch shops found in other shopping centers. You may find Barrashopping to be more of a cultural experience than an adventure in quality shopping. Very crowded on weekends.

SHOPPING STREETS

While most of Rio's major shopping is concentrated in shopping centers and malls, it does have a few major shopping streets worth exploring. Within South Rio, only one street stands out for shopping. Rua Visconde de Pirajá is its most fashionable shopping street:

❑ **Rua Visconde de Pirajá:** Located in the heart of Ipanema, this is considered to be the city's most fashionable shopping street. However, shopping realities in Rio are relative – compared to what? Compared to the rest of Rio, it's true. Compared to São Paulo and many other countries, this street leaves much to be desired. While it has some interesting shops, don't expect to find many top quality shops here. Indeed, you may find this street somewhat disappointing with its overall lack of attractive shops. It includes lots of nondescript clothing, jewelry, and drug stores as well as newsstands and banks. Nonetheless, it includes a few noted shops worth visiting in this area of the city. For example, here you'll find the headquarters workshop and showroom for the venerable gemstone dealer and jeweler, **H. Stern** (Rua Visconde de Pirajá, 490, Tel. 259-7442). Just around the corner is the company's attractive home decorative shop, **H. Stern Home** (Rua Garcia d'Ávila, 102/108, Tel. 239-7845), with its excellent selection of imported Italian glass, porcelain, and silver which is popular with many upscale local customers. Next door to H. Stern, as well as across the street from H. Stern Home, is this company's major but much smaller competitor, **Amsterdam Sauer** (Rua Visconde de Pirajá, 484, Tel. 512-9878), with its excellent selection of gemstones and jewelry. Organized similar to H. Stern – factory tour and showrooms – as well as including an interesting gemstone museum, Amsterdam Sauer attracts many tour groups each day who tour the factory and end up in its glitzy upstairs showroom. Across the street is **Victor Hugo** (Rua Visconde de Pirajá, 507, Tel. 259-9699) for nicely designed Brazilian leather handbags. If you walk east along Rua Visconde de Pirajá, you'll eventually come to a small but very exclusive handbag shop on the south side of the street and adjacent to Forum de Ipanema, **Glorinha Paranaguá** (Rua Visconde de Pirajá, 365, Tel. 267-4295). **Forum de Ipanema** at Rua Visconde de Pirajá, 351, includes several excellent jewelry shops such as **Lisht**, **Francesca Romana**, **Sabbá**, and **Wolfgrang Badofszky**. Further east, along Rua Visconde de Pirajá, is one of Rio's largest and most densely stocked bookstores, **Letras & Expressões** (Rua Visconde de Pirajá, 276, Tel. 521-6110).

MARKETS

Markets or fairs (*feiras*), especially weekend markets, are extremely popular with local residents and visitors alike. In fact, since many shops close on either Saturday or Sunday, the weekend markets function as lively centers for shopping and entertainment. Like much of Rio's shopping, the markets are primarily found in South Rio. Some of the major arts, crafts, and antique markets include:

❑ **Feirarte I or Feira Hippie (Hippie Fair):** Located at the Praça General Osorio in Ipanema, the Hippie Fair operates on Sunday from 8am to 6pm. Increasingly touristy but fun, this is one of Rio's largest and most popular arts and crafts markets. Over 150 vendors set up stalls offering everything from leather bags, belts, clothes, and jewelry to toys, stones, paintings, and T-shirts. The market is especially noted for its art section which includes hundreds of colorful paintings reflecting many local themes (scenery, flowers, samba, and *favelas*).

❑ **Babilônia Feira Hype:** Located on the grounds of the Brazilian Jockey Club (just north of Leblon), this popular arts, crafts, and clothing market operates biweekly on both Saturday and Sunday (2pm to 11pm). Nearly 200 vendors set up stalls alongside the horse track. The market also includes food vendors, music, and dance. Many people prefer this market to the more touristy Hippy Fair, although both are well worth visiting together on Saturday. The added bonus here for shoppers is to see the weekend horse races at this classic club.

❑ **Cassino Antique Fair:** Shopping Cassino Atlântico. Attached to the Hotel Sofitel Rio Palace at the southern tip of Copacabana, this popular art, antiques, jewelry, and handicraft center transforms itself into a weekend market on Saturdays (11am to 7pm). Nearly 50 exhibitors display their products on tables that occupy the walkways of this three-level shopping center.

❑ **Centro de Antiguidades Rio Design Center:** Similar to the Cassino Antique Fair, the antiques market at the Rio Design Center (Rua Ataulfo de Paiva, 280 in Leblon), with over 60 exhibitors, takes place on Sunday from 11am to 7pm. Since over 75 percent of the vendors who exhibit at the Cassino Antique Fair on Saturday also exhibit here, you may want to skip this market if you've already visited the Cassino Antique Fair on Saturday.

❑ **Feirarte da Praça do Lido:** Located at Praça do Lido in Copacabana, this craft and clothing market is open on Saturday and Sunday from 8am to 6pm. Includes 60 vendors.

❑ **do Calcadão de Copacabana:** Every Saturday and Sunday evening, from 7pm to 12midnight, in front of the Hotel Rio Othon at Avenida Atlântica, 3264, a food, clothes, and art market operates. Includes nearly 80 vendors.

❑ **Casa Shopping Center:** Barra da Tijuca. Includes a Sunday antiques market.

CENTRAL (CENTRO) RIO

While Centro has many shops geared toward the local consumer market, most shopping of interest to visitors will be found in the museums and along Centro's major antique, furniture, and collectibles streets, Rua do Senado/Rua do Lavradio.

❑ **Museum:** Most museums include a small gift shop. One of the best such shops is found at the **National Museum of Fine Arts** (Museu Nacional de Belas Artes, Av. Rio Branco, 199, Tel. 240-0068). The shop on the second floor is well stocked with arts, crafts, books, paintings, prints, T-shirts, and folk art. You'll need to pay admission (R$4) to the museum before entering this shop.

❑ **Rua do Senado/Rua do Lavradio:** Located in Centro, just west of the conical Catedral Metropolitana, these two adjoining streets comprise one of Rio's major antique and furniture centers which sometime approximate an upscale flea market. It's relatively easy and cheap (R$1) to get here from Copacabana by taking the Metro. These two streets are lined with more than 40 shops jam-packed with unique collections of antiques, furniture, and collectibles. A combination of second-hand junk shops and serious antique dealers, the shops here yield some of Rio's best buys on antiques and collectibles. Shop owners here are not into fancy window displays or good at in-store presentations. They tend to pile high! The number one shopping rule here is to go into the shop. Indeed, don't be put off by street front appearances, the lack of signs, or the fact a shop looks junky; many of these shops yield treasures for those willing to dig around and explore all sections of a shop. Since some shops lack signage, it may be difficult to find specific recommended shops. The whole area is one big treasure hunt, worthy of three to five hours of exploration.

The best way to approach this area is to just walk up and down these two streets; beginning at the intersection of these two streets, walk south along Rua do Lavradio and west along Rua do Senado. Some of our favorite shops along **Rua do Lavradio** include **Alfonso Nunes Antiquerio** (Rua do Lavradio, 60, Tel. 852-0220) with its two dusty levels of antiques, art, and collectibles, from old cabinets, chairs, and ice boxes to lamps, china, and jars; be sure to visit the second floor which includes some unique paintings and sculptures; **Emporium 100** (Rua do Lavradio, 100, Tel. 852-5904) offers furniture and many unique collectibles; **Lavradio 185 Antiquaidades** (Rua do Lavradio, 185, Tel. 242-3342) is jam-packed with good quality furniture, china, glass, lamps, paintings, sculptures, mirrors, and walking sticks (be sure to visit the second floor); **Kalebe** (Rua do Lavradio, 106a, Tel. 224-7010) for furniture, ceramics, and glass; **Velhalapa** (Rua do Lavradio, 160, Tel. 508-8836) for two floors of furniture, glass, lamps, ceramics, paintings, and paperweights; Tudo Aquié Barato (Rua do Lavradio, 178) for furniture, paintings, and china; and **Rarities** (Rua do Lavradio, 182) for an interesting collection of glass and items from India. A major section of this street has been designated as a UNESCO heritage area. As such, the facades of the old buildings are being restored to replicate the look of old Rio. On the first Saturday of each month, the street is blocked off for pedestrians, and the whole area becomes transformed into an antique and collectible market and fair with classical music, children's activities, and vendor stalls.

Rua do Senado also is lined with antiques, furniture, and collectibles shops. Running west of the intersection with Rua do Lavradio for three blocks, this area has many small shops filled with all kinds of furniture and collectibles, from chairs, tables, chests, mirrors, and lamps to paintings, china, sculptures, silver, and glassware. Some of the most interesting shops along this street include: **"Z"** (Rua do Senado, 83/34, Tel. 232-1106); **Aglaise** (Rua do Senado, 70, Tel. 242-8644); **Delrey** (Rua do Senado, 45, Tel. 252-0039); **Pedro Tinoco Do Amaral Eto** (Rua do Senado, 42, Tel. 852-9096); **Agostinho dos Santos** (Rua do Senado, 40/42, Tel.252-7049).

MARKETS

Weekend markets in Centro primarily operate on Saturday. The major such markets include:

❑ **Rio Antigo:** Located along the heritage area of Rua do Lavradio, this antique market operates the first Saturday of each month from 10am to 5pm. One section of this street is closed for pedestrians and exhibitors only. Approximately 50 dealers from nearby antique, furniture, and collectible shops display their wares. Includes street music and children's activities.

❑ **de Antiguidades:** Located at Praça 15 de Novembro (next to old tower of the Mercado Municipal), this antiques fair is held every Saturday from 10am to 5pm. Includes over 60 exhibitors.

❑ **Feira da Troca:** This antiques market operates at Rua da Assembléia and Rua Primeiro de Marco every Saturday from 9am to 5pm. Includes approximately 80 exhibitors.

LARANJEIRAS AND BOTAFOGO

Located south of Centro and north of South Rio, these two districts house a few excellent quality arts and crafts shops. We especially like a small shop called **Brumado** (Rua Das Laranjeiras, 486, Tel. 558-2275). Specializing in arts and crafts of various Indian and Amazon tribes, Brumado includes a good selection of rugs, pots, headdresses, furniture, lacework, baskets, carvings, and paddles. **Pé de Boi** (Rua Ipiranga, 55, Laranjeriras, Tel. 285-4395) includes a large, attractive, and fun selection of Brazilian folk art produced by several local artists. **Artíndia**, which is on the grounds of the Indian Museum (Museu do Índio, Rua das Palmeiras, 55, Botafogo, Tel. 286-8899, ext. 229), offers a good selection of Indian arts and crafts (baskets, bird stools, spears, paddles, headdresses) as well as books at very good prices. You'll also find several shopping opportunities at the two major sightseeing attractions to the east and west of Botafogo – Corcovado and Pão de Açucar (Sugar Loaf). Most of the shops around these two sites offer lots of arts, crafts, and T-shirts. An antiques market, **Mercado Forte**, (campus of the Universidade Federal do Rio de Janeiro, behind the Canecéo) operates in this area from 9am to 5pm and includes nearly 150 exhibitors.

BEST OF THE BEST

If you have limited shopping time in Rio, you may want to concentrate your shopping in the following shops which we found to be of exceptional quality or of particular note because of their unique offerings and service.

GEMS AND JEWELRY

❑ **H. Stern:** *Rua Visconde de Pirajá, 490 (Ipanema), Tel. 259-7442, Fax 259-1011. Website: **www.hstern.com.br** (in development). Email: tmk@hstern.com.br. Additional shops throughout Rio, especially in or next to major hotels, such as the Intercontinental and Copacabana Palace Hotels.* Welcome to one of the world's most fascinating gem and jewelry empires as well as one of the most interesting gem and jewelry tours. If you visit only one gem and jewelry store in Brazil, or perhaps even in the world, make sure it's H. Stern. This will probably be one of the major highlights of your shopping adventure in Brazil. This Ipanema shop, which actually consists of 13 floors with 600 employees, with the first three floors open to the public, is the world headquarters workshop and showroom for Brazil's largest gemstone and jewelry manufacturer and dealer. H. Stern is an integrated jeweler that controls a supply chain that begins in the mines and ends up in jewelry showrooms around the world. Employing 2,800 people in Brazil and 800 abroad in its mines, factories, design studios, and 175 outlets in 14 different countries, H. Stern handles nearly 60 percent of all Brazilian gemstones and produces nearly 20,000 pieces of jewelry each month. Nearly 90 percent of everything produced here is exported. The quality and designs are excellent, as is the reputation of H. Stern which has been in business for 55 years. The company works with the Gemological Institute of America and offers a world guarantee on its jewelry (you can exchange a piece during the first year at any H. Stern store; after that, they will value the piece and apply it toward the purchase of another H. Stern purchase). If you've ever wanted to learn about gemstones and the jewelry making process, this is one of the best places to visit. Visitors are literally taken on a free tour of the workshop – the H. Stern Gemological Tour – where they learn about the whole process of acquiring, selecting, cutting, and polishing gemstones as well as the process of designing, manufacturing, and selling jewelry. A well organized tour takes visitors through the workshop and museum and then to a huge showroom where sales people assist visitors by answering questions, showing jewelry, and closing deals. Few people can resist buying something before they leave. While much of the jewelry is expensive, the showroom does maintain a separate US$300 showcase for those who are looking for something relatively inexpensive. As you exit the showroom, you pass through H. Stern's Brazilian folk arts and crafts shop, **Folclore**, which includes many souvenirs, from sculptured semiprecious stone birds to silver, paintings, sand sculptures, ceramics, miniature charms, laces, and embroidery. Most tour groups, including cruise ship passengers, come here for the tour. Whether you plan to buy jewelry or not, visiting this factory/shop is time well spent just for learning about Brazilian gemstones and the process of designing and making jewelry. If you do decide to buy, H. Stern claims you will save about 20 percent by making your purchase in its Rio store. They certify and guarantee their gemstones and jewelry. They also will custom-make jewelry and size rings within one hour. This shop is H. Stern's manufacturing and tour center. Its marketing and financial center is in São Paulo.

❑ **Amsterdam Sauer**: *Rua Visconde de Pirajá, 484 (Ipanema), Tel. 512-9878, Fax 294-4728. Website: www.amsterdamsauer. com. Email: amsauer@ibm.net.* Gem and jewelry shoppers find shopping both convenient and competitive when they come here. Located next door to H. Stern, Amsterdam Sauer is a smaller version of H. Stern, its main competitor. It has been in operation for more than 65 years. Like H. Stern, Amsterdam Sauer has a gem and jewelry showroom, a handicraft section, and a museum. One of the real highlights here is the museum, the private collection of owner Jules Roger Sauer. It offers a wonderful display of beautiful precious stones in their natural rough stage as well as examples of tunnels and shafts found at their mines in Bahia, Goiás, and Minas Gerais. Like H. Stern, Amsterdam Sauer produces beautiful gemstones, offers nicely designed jewelry, and includes souvenirs such as birds made from semi-previous stones and "Penca" jewelry (local charms). Unlike H. Stern, Amsterdam Sauer is primarily a local company with shops in a few Brazilian cities and abroad in St. Thomas, the U.S. Virgin Islands, and Miami. You are well advised to visit both H. Stern and Amsterdam Sauer since they are very competitive. When it comes to jewelry designs and gemstone quality, Amsterdam Sauer holds it own compared to H. Stern and they are eager to compete, and undercut, their big neighbor. You'll also find branches of Amsterdam Sauer in nine other locations in Rio (Av. Atlântica next to the Copacabana Palace Hotel, Av. Rio Branco in Centro, Shopping Rio Sul, Barrashopping, Othon Palace Hotel, Meridien Hotel, Rio Palace Hotel, Caesar Park Hotel, Pão de Açúcar). Don't be shy about discounts. Salespeople can give a 10 percent discount; the manager may do better.

❑ **Akbar:** *Shopping Cassino Atlântico, Av. Atlântica, 4240/241 (Copacabana), Tel. 522-3300, Fax 522-3300. Website: www. akbar.com.br. Email: jibrahim@centroin.com.br.* Operating since 1984, this small shop produces very nice quality jewelry. The owner and designer previously worked for H. Stern and is experienced in working with English-speaking expats. He regularly works with U.S. Consulate and corporate personnel. Offers excellent quality gems and fine jewelry designs. Will do custom work with many pieces completed within 48 hours. Also wholesales gems. If you're looking for something special, whether original or copied from major jewelers, Akbar may be the perfect shop for all your jewelry needs.

❑ **Lisht:** *São Conrado Fashion Mall, Tel. 322-5779; Forum de Ipanema, Tel. 522-8618; Shopping Da Gávea, Tel. 511-4652; and Barrashopping, Tel. 431-8883. Website: www.lisht.com.br.* Produces nicely designed gold and diamond jewelry. Very contemporary and first-class. The shop at the São Conrado Fashion Mall has especially attractive displays.

❑ **Francesca Romana:** *São Conrado Fashion Mall, Tel. 322-2197, and Forum de Ipanema, Tel. 521-0877.* These popular shops offer top quality fashion jewelry at reasonable prices. Many of the designs look similar to David Yurman jewelry designs. Earrings using semi-precious stones are especially popular. Very fashionable designs.

ART

❑ **Dag Saboya:** *Shopping Cassino Atlântico, Av. Atlântica, 4240, 128, Tel. 287-1456.* Considered by many local residents to be the top dealer in Brazilian art. This relatively nondescript shop works with many of Brazil's top artists. Be sure to ask the shop personnel about their art collection.

❑ **Mauricio Pontual:** *Shopping Cassino Atlântico, Av. Atlântico, 4240, 110 Tel. 522-5810.* Offers a fine collection of Brazilian oil paintings and black and white prints.

❑ **Galeria G**: *Shopping da Gávea, R. Marquês de São Vicente, 52 Loja 2109, Tel. 274-8198. Also has a gallery at Barrashopping, Av. das Américas, 4666 Loja 132B, Tel. 431-9027.* Specializes in quality Brazilian paintings and sculptures.

❑ **Feira Hippie (Hippie Fair)**: *Praça General Osorio, Ipanema. Open Sunday, 9am to 6pm.* Includes a large selection of relatively inexpensive oils, watercolors, and prints by amateur artists. Good place to shop for souvenir art.

ANTIQUES

❑ **Arte & Antiguidade**: *Rua Siqueira Campos, 143, Tel. 235-0935.* This large antique and home decorative shop is filled with quality furniture, porcelain, religious altars and figures, paintings, chandeliers, rugs, and silver. Includes many unique pieces.

❑ **Rue Jadis Antiguidades**: *Shopping Cassino Atlântico, Av. Atlântico, 4240, 335/322, Tel. 522-3873, Fax 267-4346.* Operates two shops across the hall from each other. Includes an excellent collection of antique furniture, porcelain, lamps, tapestries, vases, Chinese chests, and pots.

❑ **Lavradio 158 Antiguidades**: *Rua do Lavradio, 158, Tel. 242-3342.* The two floors of this shop include lots of nice furniture, including marble top tables, china, glass, lamps, paintings, and sculptures. Includes art deco lamps, walking sticks, and mirrors. Most of the furniture is on the second floor.

CLOTHES

❑ **Lenny**: *São Conrado Fashion Mall, Estrada da Gávea, 899, 217, Tel. 322-2561. Open Monday to Thursday, 10am-10pm; Friday and Saturday, 10am-11pm; and Sunday, 1-10pm. Also at Shopping Rio Sul.* Offers fashionable swimwear, from bikinis to one-piece swimsuits which can be worn with skirts or coordinated *paréos*. Includes attractive fabrics and colors.

❑ **Frankie e Amaury**: *São Conrado Fashion Mall, Estrada da Gávea, 899, 216-B, Tel. 322-2561.* This attractive boutique includes women's clothes and leather accessories.

❑ **Shopping Malls**: Fashionable boutiques, trendy clothes, and sportswear can be found in abundance at the São Conrado Fashion Mall, Barrashopping, and Shopping Rio Sul.

LEATHER AND ACCESSORIES

☐ **Glorinha Paranaguá:** *Rua Visconde de Pirajáam, 365, Tel. 267-4295.* This little shop – a hole in the wall – produces some lovely handbags made with wood and straw. They are all produced in the workshop on the second floor. Very unique designs.

☐ **Victor Hugo:** *Viconde de Pirajá, 507, Tel. 259-9699; Rio Sul; Barrashopping; Rio Branco, 155; and three other locations.* Produces nicely designed leather handbags made in Brazil in attractive colors.

☐ **Santa Marinella:** *Barrashopping, Av. das Américas, 4666, loja 132-C, Tel. 431-9829; and Shopping Center Rio Sul (Tel. 275-9346).* Offers very attractively designed leather handbags.

HANDICRAFTS

☐ **Pé de Boi:** *Rua Ipiranga, 55 (Laranjeiras), Tel. 285-4395. Website: www.pedeboi.com.br. Open Monday-Saturday, 8am-7:30pm.* One of the best shops representing colorful Brazilian folk arts and crafts. Includes many nice handcrafted items from the serious to the fun – wood carvings, ceramics, prints, rugs, and some Indian pottery. Represents many different artists who produce signed pieces. The upstairs area includes rugs and pottery. Experienced in shipping abroad.

☐ **Brumado:** *Rue Das Laranjeiras, 486, Loja B (Laranjeiras), Tel. 558-2275. Open Monday-Friday, 8am-7:30pm, and Saturday, 8am-1pm.* A very small but surprising shop specializing in Indian arts and crafts from many different tribes. Includes woven Diamantina carpets, handwoven bedcovers, cushions, rugs, wood carvings, paddles, headdresses, pottery, handmade toys, and baskets. Also offers antiques, paintings, and Brazilian colonial furniture.

☐ **Artíndia:** *On grounds of Museu do Índio, Rua das Palmeiras, 55 (Botafogo), Tel. 286-8899, ext. 229. Open Monday-Saturday, 8am-7:30pm.* This museum shop offers an interesting collection of relatively inexpensive arts and crafts from various Indian tribes, including baskets, bird stools, spears, paddles, headdresses and books.

☐ **Folclore:** *Hotel Intercontinental, Av. Prefeito Mendes de Moraes, 222, São Conrado, Tel. 322-1831. Also on the ground floor of*

H.Stern, Rua Visconde de Pirajá, 490 (Ipanema), Tel. 259-7442, Fax 259-1011. Offers an interesting collection of quality Brazilian folk arts and crafts from Bahia, Santa Catarina, and North and Northeast Brazil. Includes beautiful agate sculptured birds (cockatoos and toucans), clay figurines, lace, sand sculptures, wood carvings, ceramics, silver, leather, and more.

GIFTS AND TABLEWARE

❑ **H. Stern Home:** *Rua Garcia d'Ávila, 102/108, Tel. 239-7845.* Located across the street from Amsterdam Sauer, this is H. Stern's gift and tableware shop. Its two floors are filled with beautiful glassware, silver pieces, china, and porcelain from Italy, China, and Japan. Very popular with local residents who are attracted to such imported items.

❑ **Sobotka & Co.:** *São Conrado Fashion Mall, Estrada da Gávea, 899, 106H, Tel. 422-0972.* Includes an attractive selection of crystal, glassware, and bronze pieces. Owned by Feddy's jewelry at Shopping Cassino Atlântico.

BOOKS

❑ **Letras & Expressões:** *Rua Visconde de Pirajá, 276 (Ipanema), Tel. 521-6110. Open 24 hours a day.* Its two floors are jam-packed with books, magazines, newspapers, CDs, and tobacco products.

MUSIC

❑ **Gramophone:** *Shopping Center da Gávea, Rua Marquês de São Vicente, 52, 138/139 (Gávea), Tel. 274-2495.* Excellent collection of Brazilian music, especially the major bossa-nova artists.

❑ **Gabriela:** *Shopping Center da Gávea, Rua Marquês de São Vicente, 52, 107 (Gávea), Tel. 274-3245.* A popular chain of music stores.

ACCOMMODATIONS

Rio has many good quality four- and five-star hotels. Most are found in and around the three major beach and shopping areas in South Rio: Copacabana, Ipanema, and São Conrado. You are well advised to stay in these areas since they are convenient to most of the city's top shopping, dining, sightseeing, and recreational activities.

❏ **Copacabana Palace:** *Avenida Atlântica, 1702, Rio de Janeiro CEP 22021-001, Brazil, Tel. (55 21) 548-7070, Fax (55 21) 235-7330. Website: **www.copacabanapalace.com.br**.* Situated on the promenade facing Copacabana Beach, the Copacabana Palace may just be – as their brochure suggests – the grandest hotel in South America. The hotel's facade was featured prominently and made a famous landmark in the 1933 film, *Flying Down to Rio*, starring Ginger Rogers and Fred Astaire. Having gone through extensive renovation since being acquired by Orient-Express Hotels in 1989, and listed as one of "The Leading Hotels of the World," the Copacabana Palace sparkles like a gem while retaining its traditional look and feel. Although the entrance lobby is surprisingly small, it functions well. The hotel's 226 guestrooms and suites (148 in the main building and 78 in the Annex) are spacious. Decorated in a style both classic and cozy, they provide the utmost in comfort. All have been soundproofed both internally and externally; a new telecommunications system installed; air conditioning upgraded; modern bathrooms installed which offer all amenities expected in a luxury hotel. An executive floor was created housing 26 apartments and suites complete with an executive lounge and kitchen. Suite designs include collections of Brazilian mahogany inlaid with Brazilian agates. High tech appointments include compact disc players, video cassette recorders, televisions that are brought into view by a remote operated lift when in use, but otherwise tuck discreetly out of sight; and fax and computer modems can be plugged directly into telephone lines. The two Penthouse Suites each offer over 100 square meters of elegant space and can be joined to provide up to 220 square meters. With butler service and use of their own private swimming pool, guests in the Penthouse Suites enjoy the ultimate in luxury. The concierge staff are extremely helpful to all guests – whether or not they are registered in one of the suites.

The hotel's *Cipriani Restaurant* is a sophisticated Italian restaurant reminiscent of the Copacabana's sister Hotel Cipriani in Venice. All dishes are freshly prepared for each diner. Even the pasta is made on a daily basis. The less formal, *Pergula Restaurant*, serves afternoon tea poolside, as well as breakfast, lunch and light snacks either inside or on the pool terrace throughout the day. Sunday brunch at *Pergula* is a Rio tradition. A private semi-Olympic-size pool,

Rio's largest, offers a large area for sunbathing or walk across the promenade to the beach. New rooftop tennis court and new Health Club. Water sports nearby include surfing and jet skiing, cruising and snorkeling around the off-shore islands. Golf, beach volleyball, and many other sports available. Convention center and meeting facilities.

❑ **Hotel Inter-Continental Rio:** *Av. Prefeito Mendes de Moraes, 222 São Conrado 22610 090, Rio de Janeiro, Brazil, Tel. (55 21) 323-2200, Fax (55 21) 322-5500. Website: **www.intercon t-i.com**.* The Inter-Continental's 483 guestrooms include 40 suites and 20 poolside rooms; 29 Club Inter-Continental rooms and 23 Club Inter-Continental Suites. 62 guestrooms are non-smoking rooms and 2 rooms are equipped with facilities for the disabled. Most all rooms have balconies overlooking the ocean. Tapestries by local artists decorate guestrooms which are tastefully and comfortably decorated. Expected amenities are provided. The 31 business rooms offer multifunctional equipment with fax, printer, scanner, and photocopier. A large working desk, ergonomic chair, and coffee/tea making facilities are extras provided in business rooms. Club Inter-Continental is located on the 15th and 17th floors; the Club rooms offer upgraded amenities, access to the Club Lounge where complimentary breakfast and afternoon tea are served. Private check-in and check-out, complimentary secretarial services and meeting room for up to six people are also available. *Alfredo di Roma,* the formal restaurant, serves Italian cuisine to the accompaniment of live piano music. *A Varanda*, an informal restaurant serves buffets, while *Captain Cook Sea House* serves seafood by the pool. The snack bar serves fast food.

This is a resort hotel that is technically in the city, though guests need to take taxis or the shuttle service to and from the city center. Standing on its own beachfront, offering 3 pools, and with a golf course right next door and access to a second golf course available to guests along with 3 tennis courts and a jogging trail by the beach and an upscale shopping mall, São Conrado Fashion Mall, next door as well, most guests spend most of their time enjoying their seaside resort. Business Center; Health/Fitness Facilities; Convention and Banquet Facilities.

❑ **Le Meridien Copacabana:** *Avenida Atlântica, 1020, Copacabana, Rio de Janeiro, Brazil, Tel. (55 21) 546-0840, Fax (55 21) 542-6739. Website: **www.meridien-br.com**.* Located across the street from Copacabana Beach, Le Meridien has 441 guestrooms and 55 suites. 90% of the guestrooms have an ocean-view, and from the higher floors (37 floors) the view can be stunning. Guestrooms provide all amenities expected in a luxury hotel. Non-smoking floors available. Recognized as one of the best restaurants in South America, *Le Saint Honoré* has won numerous culinary awards and affords a magnificent 37th floor view of Copacabana Beach and Corcovado mountain with its statue of Christ the Redeemer. *Restaurant Café De La Paix* is located on the same level as the pool and also provides a view of the beach. The cuisine reflects the heritage of the Mediterranean and Provence. *Le St. Tropez*, located on the pool terrace, on the 4th floor, offers a variety of light dishes with the accent on salads and sandwiches. Business Center.

❑ **Caesar Park Ipanema:** *Avenida Viera Souto, 460, Cep 22420-000, Rio de Janeiro, RJ, Brazil, Tel. (55 21) 525-2525, Fax (55 21) 521-6000 or toll-free from U.S. or Canada 800-343-7821. Website: www.caesarpark-rio.com.* A member of "The Leading Hotels of the World," Caesar Park Ipanema is one of the top hotels in Rio. Located between the sea and the mountains in an elegant neighborhood surrounded by upscale shops and near the business center of the city, the Caesar Park Ipanema is known for its luxury accommodations and quality of its services. The 221 guestrooms and suites, each with a sea view, are decorated in a style both classic and comfortable and provide the amenities expected in a luxury hotel. The restaurant, *Galani*, serves a range of cuisines and is open daily for breakfast, lunch, and dinner. Located on the top floor, *Galani* provides dazzling view over Ipanema and Leblon to complement the restaurant's atmosphere. Courtesy parking is available for guests. Health Club with massage and sauna. Pool for exclusive use of guests with lifeguard and security extending to the beach. Business Center; Conference and Banquet Facilities.

❑ **Carlton Rio Atlântica:** *Avenida Atlântica, 2964, Copacabana 22070, Rio de Janeiro, Brazil, Tel. (55 21) 548-6332, Fax (55 21) 255-6410. Website: www.rioatlanta.com.br.* Located across from the beach, the Carlton Rio Atlântica has 108 guestrooms and 120 suites. Some rooms have sea views and all suites offer views of the Atlantic. Ocean facing rooms have balconies. *Ao Ponto* Restaurant offers international and typical cuisine, with menus signed by its French Chef François Sierra. The Rio Atlântica is the first hotel in Rio to achieve the ISO 9002 Certificate for Quality of Services. From the

swimming pool area there is a view over the whole of Copacabana Beach. Restaurant; Health and Fitness Center; Business
Center; Meeting and Banquet Facilities.

❑ **Marriott Rio de Janeiro:** *Avenida Atlântica, 2600, Copacabana, Rio de Janeiro, RJ, Brazil, Tel. (55 21) 545-6500, Fax (55
21) 545-6555 or toll-free from U.S. or Canada 800-228-9290.
Website: www.marriott.com.* Scheduled to open in April,
2001, the Marriott Rio will be the newest luxury hotel in
Copacabana. Its 245 guestrooms which include 16 suites, will
feature all the expected and up-to-date amenities. The *Casual
Restaurant*, with an ocean view, features Mediterranean
cuisine and regional specialities. An outdoor pool and sun
terrace on the rooftop provide a view. The Fitness Center,
sauna and Jacuzzi are also on the rooftop. Business Center;
Convention and Banquet Facilities.

You'll find several other hotels throughout the city. For a
quick reference, visit these three websites:

www.brazil.org.uk
www.rio.rj.gov.br/riotur
www.ipanema.com

The Ipanema.com site allows you to make reservations online
with most hotels in Rio.
    Most major hotels in Rio also have their own websites. In
addition to the above hotels, check out these hotels via their
websites:

Arpoador Inn:	*www.ipanema.com/hotel/arpoador_inn.htm*
Atlântico Copacabana:	*www.copacabana.com.br*
Astória Copacabana:	*www.astoria.com.br*
Califórnia Othon Classic:	*www.hoteis-othon.com.br*
Canadá:	*www.sites.uol.com.br/hotel.canada*
Castro Alves Othon Travel:	*www.hoteisothon.com.br*
Copa Sul:	*www.copasul.com.br*
Copacabana Mar:	*www.copacabanamar.com.br*
Copacabana Praia:	*www.copacabanapraiahotel.com.br*
Everest Park:	*www.everest.com.br*
Everest Rio:	*www.everest.com.br*
Excelsior Copacabana:	*www.windsorhotels.com.br*

Glória:	*www.hotelgloriario.com.br*
Grandville Ouro Verde:	*www.grandville.com.br*
Lancaster Othon Travel:	*www.hoteisothon.com.br*
Leblon Palace:	*www.leblonpalace.com.br*
Leme Othon Palace:	*www.hoteisothon.com.br*
Luxor Aeroporto:	*www.luxor-hotels.com*
Luxor Continental:	*www.luxor-hotels.com.br*
Luxor Copacabana:	*www.luxor-hotels.com/copacabana*
Luxor Regente:	*www.luxor-hotels.com/regente*
Mar Ipanema:	*www.maripanema.com.br*
Marina All Suite:	*www.hotelmarina.com.br*
Merlin Copacabana:	*www.hotelmerlin.com.br*
Mirado Rio:	*www.hotelmirador.com.br*
Novo Mundo:	*www.hotelnovomundorio.com.br*
Olinda Othon Classic:	*www.hoteis-othon.com.br*
Plaza Copacabana:	*www.windsorhotels.com.br*
Praia Ipanema:	*www.praiaipanema.com*
Premier Copacabana:	*www.premier.com.br*
Real Palace:	*www.realpalachotelrj.com.br*
Rio Internacional:	*www.riointernacional.com.br*
Rio Othon Palace:	*www.hoteis-othon.com.br*
Ritz:	*www.ritzhotel.com.br*
Rondônia Palace:	*www.hotelrondonia.com.br*
Savoy Othon Travel:	*www.hoteisothon.com.br*
Sheraton Rio Hotel/Towers:	*www.sheraton-rio.com*
Sofitel Rio Palace:	*www.accorbrasil.com.br*
Sol Ipanema:	*www.solipanema.com.br*
Trocadero Othon Travel:	*www.hoteisothon.com.br*
Windsor Palace:	*www.windsorhotels.com.br*

RESTAURANTS

If you love to combine shopping with dining – "lifestyle shopping" – Rio will not disappoint you. Dining in Rio is very much a social event that starts late and may take two to three hours to complete, including long lunches. As one might expect from a good party city, Rio boasts many excellent restaurants. While few are truly outstanding, and many are overrated, some restaurants, such as Columbo and Antiquarius, are very memorable places to dine. Many places with Brazilian cuisine and buffets serve huge portions. Representing everything from the Carioca's traditional *feijoada* dish (soupy mix of beans and meat), *rodizios* (all you can eat skewered barbecued meats with buffet dishes), and seafood to Portuguese, Spanish, French, Italian, and Japanese restaurants, Rio is a fun place for dining out. Some of Rio's best restaurants include:

BRAZILIAN

❑ **Porcão:** *Rua Barão da Torre, 218 (Ipanema), Tel. 522-0999; and Av. Armando Lombardi, 591 (Bara da Tijuca), Tel. 492-2001. Open 11:30am - 1am.* Attentive waiters roam the aisles of this lively rodizio-style steak house and serve sizzling barbecued meats on long skewers at your table when told to do so through the traditional green and red wood cube signaling system.

❑ **Geraes:** *Rua do Ouvidor 26-28 (Centro), Tel. 242-8610. Serves lunch only but open in the evening for drinks and music.* Offers traditional Brazilian dishes (beans, bacon, pork sausage) in an attractive setting.

❑ **Casa da Feijoada:** *Rua Prudente de Morais, 10 (Ipanema), Tel. 523-4994. Open 12noon to 12midnight.* Serves the Carioca's traditional dish, *feijoada*, which is a mixture of beans and meats. Diners order meat and side dishes to go with the *feijoada*. Drink and dessert included in the fixed price menu.

❑ **Barra Grill:** *Av. Ministro Ivan Lins, 314 (Barra da Tijuca), Tel. 493-6060. Open 11am to 2am.* Attentive waiters serve excellent rodizio-style meats at your table. Includes a huge buffet spread to accompany the never-ending array of 12 tasty meats – beef, lamb, chicken, pork, ribs, and pork sausage. Provides a free shuttle from the restaurant if you have difficulty getting a taxi late at night.

❑ **Alvaro's Bar:** *São Conrado Fashion Mall, 2nd floor, Estrada da Gávea.* If you're shopping at the São Conrado Fashion Mall, this is a good place to stop for lunch. Its expansive menu includes many tasty Brazilian dishes. Be prepared for huge portions.

❑ **Marius Ipanema:** *Rua Francisco Otaviano, 96 (Ipanema), Tel. 521-0500. Open 11:45am - 1pm.* Local steak house serving *churraso*, rodizio-style meats.

❑ **Bar do Arnaudo:** *Largo do Guimarães, R Almte Alexandria, 316 (Centro, Santa Teresa), Tel. 252-7246. Open Tuesday-Saturday, 12noon - 10pm, and Sunday, 11am-6pm.* This rather plain northeast Brazilian restaurant serves many excellent dishes, such as *carne do sol* (sun-dried meat), *pirão de bode* (goat meat soup), and *feijão de corda* (brown beans and herbs). Inexpensive.

PORTUGUESE

❏ **Antiquarius:** *Rua Artistides Epínola, 19 (Leblon), Tel. 294-1049.* This award-winning restaurant is one of Brazil's very best Portuguese restaurants. Famous for its leg of lamb (*perna de cordeiro*) and cod fish (*bacalhau lagareira*). While everything here is generally excellent, the real special treat is the octopus (*polvo à portuguesa*) which is simply outstanding! Also try the seafood rice and Brazilian moquecca. Decor includes many antiques in display cases which are for sale.

FRENCH

❏ **Troisgros:** *Rua Custódio Serrão, 62 (Jardim Botânico), Tel. 537-8582. Open 12noon to 3:30pm; and 7:30pm to 12:30am; Saturday 7:30pm to 12:30am. Closed Sunday.* Considered by many of the city's top concierges to be Rio's best French restaurant. This small but charming restaurant serves many inventive dishes. While somewhat risky for picky eaters, the special three-course "Chef's Surprise" is usually an excellent choice – often the envy of others sharing your table.

❏ **Le Saint Honoré:** *Hotel Le Méridien, Av. Atlântica, 1020, 37th floor (Copacabana), Tel. 546-0880. Open 7pm to 12 midnight; closed Sunday.* This popular restaurant serves excellent French cuisine. While the menu changes every season, look for such classics as the ravioli, catfish, lamb ribs, and duck. Added bonus is the excellent view of Copacabana Beach.

ITALIAN

❏ **Cipriani:** *Copacabana Palace Hotel, Av. Atlântica 1702 (Copacabana), Tel. 545-8747. Open 12:30pm to 3pm and 8pm to 1am.* This elegant fine dining restaurant, with a pianist playing selections from the foyer, serves excellent contemporary Italian cuisine, especially pastas and lamb. Offers two tasting menus.

❏ **Quadrifoglio:** *Rua J.J. Seabra, 19 (Jardim Botânico), Tel. 294-1433. Open 12:30pm to 3:30pm and 7:30pm to 1am; Saturday,*

7:30 to 1am. This elegant restaurant/house serves many creative Italian dishes which constantly change. Good choices include ravioli stuffed with apple puree, risottos, and barbecued duck breast with raisins. Tempting desserts.

❑ **Alho & Óleo:** *Rua Buarque de Macedo, 13 (Flamengo), Tel. 558-33-45; and Rua Barao da Torre, 348 (Ipanema), Tel. 523-2703. Open 12noon - 1am.* Somewhat eclectic, this popular restaurant offers a nice range of inventive dishes, including many Italian specialties and seafood. Known for its filet mignon, ravioli of yam, and lamb ribs.

SEAFOOD

❑ **Satyricon:** *Rua Barão da Torre, 192 (Ipanema), Tel. 521-0627. Open Monday, 6pm - 2am and Tuesday - Sunday, 12noon - 12 midnight.* This well appointed Italian seafood restaurant offers many excellent dishes. The house specialty is *bacalhau*, a fish baked in rock salt and uncovered and served at your table. Also includes other Italian dishes as well as Japanese specialties (sushi bar). Popular with celebrities.

❑ **Mediterrâneo:** *Rua Prudente de Moraes, 1810 (Leblon/Ipanema), Tel. 259-4696.* One of our very favorite restaurants in Rio. This charming corner neighborhood restaurant is a hidden treasure for lunch or dinner. Serves wonderful seafood dishes that you'll want to come back for again and again. On a nice day, get an outside table where you can overlook the street and watch all the people and traffic pass by. Lunch here can easily become a two-hour affair.

❑ **Grottamare:** *Rua Gomes Carneiro, 132 (Ipanema), Tel. 523-1596. Open Monday - Friday, 7pm-1am, and Saturday and Sunday, 12noon to 1am.* Nothing fancy here – just lots of good seafood in a rustic setting. Expect large portions.

INTERNATIONAL

❑ **Columbo:** *Rua Gonçalves Dias, 32 (Centro), Tel. 323-2300. Open Monday - Friday, 8am-7pm.* If you're in the Centro area, don't miss this one (a little difficult to find since it's a huge place located down a narrow alley), especially the well appointed upstairs dining room with beautiful stained glass and organ music. This architectural masterpiece is a popular gathering place for snacks, pastries, and drinks (downstairs café counters) and an international buffet lunch (upstairs dining room). One of the most interesting and memorable (architecturally) restaurants in Brazil. The food is okay, too.

SEEING THE SITES

In addition to shopping and dining, there's lots to see and do in Rio to easily occupy a full week. Major sightseeing can be done in three days and easily integrated into one's shopping plans.

Most of Rio's interesting museums, churches, and architecture are found in the downtown or Centro area. Beaches and the famous hills for viewing Rio are found farther south.

Most sightseeing involves climbing to high points to get panoramic views of the area and visiting museums, churches, and beaches. Because Rio is such a visually seductive place, from the mountains to the beaches, you'll probably want to do what millions of other people have done before you – see the city from its highest points, Corcovado and Pão de Açucar (Sugar Loaf). You can even get a higher view by hiring a helicopter or hang-gliding or parasailing off of Pedra da Gávea near São Conrado.

PANORAMIC VIEWS OF CITY

❑ **Morro do Corcovado:** *Rua Cosme Velho, 513 (Cosme Velho), Tel. 558-1329. Open 9am - 6pm.* Access by car (R$5 per car and R$5 per person) or tram (R$18 per person). The tram departs every 20 to 30 minutes. For the best view, sit on the right side of the tram as it climbs the hill. Expect to be photographed in the tram and later find your photo on plates which will be offered for sale to you later – a rather tacky souvenir reminder of your tram trip to the top. Built in 1931, this impressive landmark, a huge cement statue of Christ the Redeemer with arms outstretched, is one of Rio's major symbols. It's most impressive when viewed from a distance. Rising 710 meters above sea level, the statute itself is 38 meters tall and weighs 1,145 tons. Be prepared to climb 222 steps to the base of the statute from where you will get spectacular views of the city from several levels and vantage points. Indeed, Morro do Corcovado competes with Pão de Açucar (Sugar Loaf) as having the best view of the city and the rainforest below. A very popular site, be prepared for heavy crowds throughout the day. The crowds reach their peak when the tour buses visit, which is usually 10-11am and 2-3pm. If you want to avoid the crowds, visit early morning (9am) or late afternoon (4pm). You'll find numerous souvenir shops and cafes at the top. Be sure to take your camera since you'll have some spectacular views of the city and rainforest from this unique vantage point.

❑ **Pão de Açucar (Sugar Loaf):** *Avenida Pasteur, 520 (Urca), Tel. 541-3737. Open 8am - 10pm.* Access by cable car only (R$18 per person). This picture postcard hill is another great symbol of Rio. The site consists of two hills, linked by a 1,330 meter long cable car ride, which offer spectacular views of the city and surrounding area. Many visitors find the views from these two hills to be better than from Morro do Corcovado – a terrific photo opportunity. The first hill is Morro da Urca (Urca's Hill) which stands at 220 meters. The second hill is Sugar Loaf at 397 meters. Cable cars linking the two hills depart every 20-30 minutes and carry 70 passengers each on a 6-minute ride. They are often very crowded and may require long waits. Visitors are well advised to arrive by 9am or after 4pm in order to avoid the tour bus crowds. You may want to visit in the evening to see the sunset as well as view the city's sparkling lights, a very romantic setting. Expect to spend 1½ to 2 hours visiting this attraction because of the cable car waits. The stop between Morro da Urca and Sugar Loaf includes a restaurant and gift shop.

BUILDINGS

❑ **Theatro Municipal:** *Praça Floriano, 210 (Centro), Tel. 297-551. Open Monday to Friday, 9am - 5pm.* Completed in 1909, this ornate theater with its marble, mosaics, murals, stained glass, and wood inlaid floors is modeled after the Paris Opera House. It's well worth taking a tour (R$3 per person) of the building which can be very informative and time consuming. The theater's famous restaurant, Café do Theatro Salão Assirio, which is located just inside the front entrance, is rather kitschy – more a cultural experience than an experience in fine dining.

❑ **Biblioteca Nacional:** *Avenida Rio Branco, 219 (Centro), Tel. 262-8255. Open Monday to Friday, 9am - 8pm, and Saturday, 9am - 3pm.* This beautiful neoclassic, art deco-style building, constructed in 1910, houses the largest national library in Latin America. Includes many rare books.

❑ **Aqueduto da Carioca (Arcos da Lapa):** *Praça Cardeal Câmara* (Centro, near Catedral Metropolitana). This landmark white aqueduct with huge double arcades, constructed in 1750 to transport water from the Carioca River to residents of Santa Teresa District, now functions as a station and viaduct for the charming tram that transverses the Santa Teresa District. One of the few surviving colonial structures that gives the city some great character.

MUSEUMS

❑ **Museu Nacional de Belas Artes:** *Av. Rio Branco, 199 (Centro), Tel. 240-0068. Open Tuesday to Friday, 10am - 6pm, and Saturday and Sunday, 2-6pm.* Located opposite the Theatro Municipal and housed in one of Rio's beautiful old French-style buildings, this fine arts museum houses paintings of major Brazilian and foreign painters, including Picasso. A separate room is devoted to the works of French sculptor Auguste Rodin. Shop on second floor offers a good collection of arts, crafts, books, paintings, prints, T-shirts, and folk art.

❑ **Museu Chara do Céu:** *Rua Murtinho Nobre, 93 (Santa Teresa), Tel. 507-1932. Open Wednesday to Monday, 12noon - 5pm. Admission R$2.* Also known as the Museum of the Small Farm of the Sky, this museum is a pleasant surprise in the middle of a quiet residential area of cobblestone streets. Housed in the former residence of Raymundo de Castro Maya, a famous patron of the arts, this museum displays a lovely collection of furniture, paintings, and collectibles. It includes paintings by many internationally renowned artists such as Monet, Matisse, Picasso, and Dalí as well as leading Brazilian artists. Many furniture items are from China. Next door is the interesting ruins of a five-level house, the Parque das Ruinas (open Wednesday, Friday, and Saturday, 10am - 10pm and Sunday, 10am - 5pm). If you climb the reinforced steel starts to the top, you'll be rewarded with one of the best views of Rio. Look for special exhibitions and shows here.

❑ **Museu Histórico Nacional:** *Praça Marechal Âncora (Centro), Tel. 550-9266. Open Tuesday to Friday, 10am - 5:30pm, and Saturday and Sunday, 2pm - 6pm. Admission R$3.* Includes numerous displays portraying Brazil's history, from its discovery to its proclamation as a republic. Covers rubber, coffee, and sugar cane industries along with interesting items from the imperial family.

❑ **Museu Histórico da República:** *Rua do Catete, 153 (Flamengo), Tel. 285-6350. Open Tuesday to Friday, 12noon - 5pm, and Saturday and Sunday, 2pm - 5pm. Admission R$3 (free on*

Wednesday). Housed in the former presidential palace (Palácio do Catete, 1866 to 1960), this museum showcases Brazil's presidential history. Includes furniture, decorations, accessories, and collectibles from this period.

❑ **Museu do Índio:** *Rua das Palmerias, 55 (Botafogo), Tel. 286-8899. Open Tuesday to Friday, 10am - 5:30pm, and Saturday and Sunday, 1-5pm.* Showcases nearly 15,000 Indian artifacts, including baskets, ceramics, and masks. Compound also houses the National Indian Foundation, a reproduction of a Guaranis Indian hut, and a nice arts and crafts shop.

❑ **Museu Internacional de Arte Naïf:** *Rua Cosme Velho, 561 (Cosme Velho), Tel. 205-8612. Open Tuesday to Friday, 10am - 6pm, and Saturday and Sunday, 12noon - 6pm.* This attractive gallery displays the works of more than 500 Brazilian and foreign self-taught artists (art naïf) – one of the world's largest collections of primitive (naive) paintings with over 8,000 works of art on display. Includes a small shop.

❑ **Museu Carmen Miranda:** *Avenida Rui Barbosa, 560 (Flamengo), Tel. 551-2597. Open Monday to Friday, 11am - 5pm, and weekends, 10am - 4pm. Admission R$1.* This is the museum of Brazil's famous actress from the 1930s to the 1950s, Carmen Miranda. Includes interesting displays of her signature hats, clothes, and shoes as well as magazine clippings, movie posters, and music. Recreates the atmosphere of a flamboyant cultural period in Brazilian history.

CHURCHES

❑ **Catedral Metropolitana:** *Rua dos Arcos, 54 and Av. República do Chile, 245 (Centro), Tel. 240-2669. Open daily 7am - 5:30pm.* Completed in 1979, this distinctive cone-shaped cathedral is 80 meters tall and can accommodate a gathering of 20,000 people. Located near the old aqueduct and antique district, the cathedral dominates the skyline in this area of the city. It's worth visiting the interior of the cathedral to see the beautiful stained glass windows that run from the floor to the dome and the huge figure of Christ suspended by steel cables.

❑ **Convento de Santo Antônio:** *Largo da Carioca, 5 (Centro), Tel. 262-0129. Open Monday and Wednesday to Friday, 8am - 6pm; Tuesday, 6am - 7:30pm; and Saturday and Sunday, 8am - 5pm.* Originally constructed in 1620 as a Franciscan convent, this is one of Rio's oldest churches which also played an important role during the colonial period. Complex consists of three buildings.

❑ **Mosteiro de São Bento:** *Rua Dom Gerardo, 68 (Centro), Tel. 291-7122. Open Monday to Friday, 7-11am and 2:30-6pm; Saturday, 7:15am, and Sunday, 10am.* This baroque-style church was originally built in 1669. Includes a gorgeous carved altar, silver chandeliers, and painted ceilings. The Sunday mass is usually accompanied by Gregorian chants.

BEACHES

Rio boasts several excellent beaches, but some are polluted and thus the waters should be avoided. The best beaches are found south of the Centro area:

❑ **Flamengo:** Good for sunbathing but polluted waters.

❑ **Botafogo:** Nicely located for views of Corcovado and Sugar Loaf but polluted waters.

❑ **Copacabana:** This is where the action is, complete with restaurants, bars, kiosks, and beachfront activities. Great beach and lots of crowds.

❑ **Ipanema:** Another great beach complete with crowds and all the beach amenities required for the "beautiful people."

❑ **Leblon:** Located next to Ipanema, this nice beach is less crowded than Ipanema and Copacabana.

❑ **São Conrado:** Nice uncrowded beach which also is good for surfing. Also, a landing area for hang-gliders.

❑ **Pepino:** Just west of São Conrado Beach, Pepino Beach is the landing spot for many hang-gliders and parasailors who take off from the cliffs above, Pedra da Gávea.

❑ **Barra da Tijuca:** Located along the popular southwest suburb of Barra da Tijuca and continues for 12 kilometers as Recreio dos Bandeirantes. Popular with surfers but several sections are dangerous.

OTHER POPULAR ATTRACTIONS

❏ **Tram ride:** *Rua Lélio Gama, next to the Aqueduto da Carioca (Centro), Tel. 240-5709. Operates from 6am to 11pm. Costs R$.60.* Departing every 15 minutes, this pleasant open-air tram takes riders into the charming Santa Teresa District with its steep cobblestone streets and delightful bars, restaurants, and museums.

❏ **Parks:** Rio boasts one of the two largest urban rainforests in the world (Singapore is the second such city). As a result, its parks are lush with vegetation. If you enjoy parks, be sure to visit **Jardim Botânico** (Rua Jardim Botânico, 920, north of Leblon, Tel. 274-4888, open 8am-5pm, R$4) with its more than 8,000 species of plants, and **Jardim Zoológico** (Quinta da Boa Vista, São Cristóvão, Tel. 569-2024, open Tuesday to Sunday, 9am - 4:30pm, R$4) with its more than 2,000 animals.

❏ **Hang-gliding and parasailing:** If you stay in or visit the São Conrado and Pepino Beach areas, you'll see numerous hang-gliders and parasailors gracing the sky after leaping off of the beautiful cliffs of Pedra da Gávea. For information on hang-gliding, contact Just Fly (Tel. 208-9822, Cell 9985-7540, or email: flycelani@ax.apc.org).

❏ **Helicopter rides:** If you want a truly spectacular view of Rio, take a 7 to 30 minute helicopter ride. Rides cost anywhere from R$40 per person for 7 minutes to R$200 per person for 30 minutes (minimum of two passengers). Helicopters depart from Urca and Lagoa Rodrigo de Freitas. For information and reservations, contact Helisight (Tel. 511-2141).

❏ **Favela Tour:** Beyond Rio's seeming facade of prosperity lies a great deal of poverty and crime. Indeed, Rio is home to nearly 550 *favelas* which are basically shantytowns with stereotypical reputations for poverty and violence. While most visitors avoid such areas, a group now takes visitors on an interesting tour of the largest *favelas* in Brazil, Vila Canoas and Rocinha. The tour takes half a day (departs at 9am or 2pm). Participants visit a school, handicraft center, and other community works as well as meet the friendly people. A great way to see *favelas* up close and dispel numerous myths about these places. For more information, contact Favela Tour, Tel. 322-2727 or Cell 9989-0074.

ENTERTAINMENT

Rio's very active nightlife is synonymous with music, dance, and shows. Bars, discos, and nightclubs are plentiful. However, the highlight for many visitors is to visit a colorful and exuberant samba school or attend a Brazilian musical dance performance.

SAMBA AND CARNIVAL

Samba schools, many of which are located near *favelas* and in working class neighborhoods and disproportionately draw participants from the surrounding area, prepare Carnival participants for the ultimate entertainment highlight of the year – the Carnival procession in either February or March:

❑ **Samba schools:** Many visitors enjoy visiting a samba school during their stay in Rio. The best times to do this is between November and February when the various schools are rehearsing for Carnival. Two of the best shows for tourists are at **Beija Flor** (Rua Pracinha Wallace Paes Leme 1025, Nilópolis, Tel. 791-1353) and **Plataborma** (Rua Adalberto Ferreira, 32, Leblon, Tel. 274-4022); they offer nightly samba and dinner shows (call to check on times – dinner often starts at 8pm and the show starts at 10pm). Many samba schools have rehearsal shows on Saturday night (8, 10, or 11pm) and charge admission fees (R$5-10). Rio's most popular samba schools are **Estação Primeira da Mangueira** (Rua Visconde de Niterói, 1072, Mangueira, Tel. 567-4637) and **Imperatriz Leopoldinense** (Rua Professor Lacê, 235, Ramos, Tel. 560-8037). Also check out **Acadêmicos do Salgueiro** (Rua Silva Teles, 104, Andarai, Tel. 238-5564), **Caprichosos de Pilares** (Ruados Faleiros, I, Pilares, Tel. 594-5755), and **Grande Rio** (Rua Almirante Barroso, 5/6, Duque de Caxias, Tel. 775-8422). Several other places throughout Rio offer evening samba entertainment. Check with your hotel concierge for times and places.

❑ **Carnival:** Rio is synonymous with the annual carnival, a four-day extravagance that takes place in February or March. Various samba schools compete with colorful floats and elaborately dressed dancers in a spectacular annual parade. The action centers on Avenida Rio Branco in Centro on Fat Sunday and Fat Monday. If you plan to be in Rio during this time, be sure to make hotel reservations several months in advance since this is the most crowded time of year. For more information on Carnival, visit these two websites: ***www.love-rio.com/samba*** and ***www.ipanema.com***.

BARS AND NIGHTCLUBS

Cold beers, snacks, and conversation seem to be the order of the day, and night, in many of Rio's many small bars and beachfront eateries. Some of Rio's most popular entertainment establishments include this assortment of bars and nightclubs:

❑ **Bar Barota de Ipanema:** *Rua Vinícius de Morais, 39 (Ipanema), Tel. 267-575. Open Sunday to Tursday, 11:30am - 1am, and Friday and Saturday, 11:30am - 1:30am.* Looking for inspiration? Maybe lightning will strike twice at this bar. This famous bar supposedly inspired Tom Jobim and Vinicius de Moraes, who saw a beautiful young brunette, to write *The Girl From Ipanema*.

❑ **Bar Luiz:** *Rua da Carioca, 39 (Centro), Tel. 262-6900. Open Monday to Saturday, 11am - midnight.* For more than 100 years this bar has served as a popular watering hole. Frequented by artists and intellectuals.

❑ **Barril 1800:** *Avenida Vieira Souto, 110 (Ipanema), Tel. 523-0085. Open 9am - 2am.* This popular beachfront drinking establishment is a great place to watch the sunset while enjoying a cold beer and snacks.

❑ **Bofetada:** *Rua Farme de Amoedo, 87-A (Ipanema), Tel. 522-9526. Open 7am - 4am.* Patrons of this small but popular Portuguese bar and eatery spill out onto the sidewalk as they enjoy cold beers and conversation. Serves excellent seafood upstairs.

❑ **Canecão:** *Avenida Venceslau Brás, 215 (Botafogo), Tel. 543-1241. Open 10am - 10pm. R$15-50. Open Friday and Saturday, 10:30pm; Sunday, 9pm.* Rio's largest nightclub with popular musicians playing MPB.

❑ **Hipódromo:** *Praça Santos Dumont, 108 (Gávea), Tel. 274-9720. Open 8am - 4am.* Popular gathering place for young people. Especially crowded on Monday evening. Serves good food.

❑ **Mistura Fiona:** *Avenida Borgest de Medeiros, 3207 (Lagoa), Tel. 537-2844. Open 12noon - 3am. R$20.* Pleasant setting for this popular jazz and Latin American music club. Many top entertainers perform here. Good restaurant. Piano bar upstairs.

❑ **Sôbre as Ondas:** *Avenida Atlântica, 3432 (Copacabana), Tel. 522-1216. Open 6pm - 3am.* Popular dance floor for bossanova, samba, and MPB (Música Popular Brasileira). Good view of beachfront. Includes a restaurant, Terraço Atlântico.

ARTS AND CULTURE

Despite Rio's reputation for its lively samba schools, bars, and nightclubs, it also offers many opportunities to experience the classic performing arts, from orchestras and theaters to dance performances. Most of these performances are held in the following places:

❑ **Theatro Municipal:** *Praça Floriano (Centro), Tel. 544-2900.* Copied after the Paris Opera House and constructed in 1909, the Municipal Theater is Rio's major center for the performing arts. It operates its own ballet and opera companies. Its beautiful 2,400-seat theater is the setting for popular opera, dance, theatrical, and orchestra performances which regularly take place from April to December, the theater's official season. Its ballet toupe hosts an international ballet festival in April and May. If you can't attend a performance, at least try to take a tour of this lovely building and theater (see earlier discussion of "Buildings" under "Seeing the Sites").

❑ **Centro Cultural Banco do Brasil:** *Rua 1 de Março 66 (Centro), Tel. 808-2000. Website: **www.BancoBrasil.com.br**. Open Tuesday to Sunday, 12noon - 8pm.* This is Rio's cultural center which offers interesting art exhibits, theatrical performances, a library (100,000+ volumes), three video rooms, permanent currency exhibit ("Brazil Through Currency"), a gift shop, and free concerts at noontime. Its two theaters and auditorium seat more than 450 people.

❑ **Metropolitan:** *Av. Ayrton Senna 3000 (Barra da Tijuca), Tel. 385-0516 (tickets) or Tel. 285-3773 (schedule).* Located in the Via Parque shopping complex, this 4,500-seat performance center is used for many theatrical, musical, and dance performances.

❑ **Fundacão Casa França-Brasil:** *Rua Visconde de Itaborai, 78 (Centro), Tel. 253-5366. Open Tuesday to Sunday, 10am - 8pm.*

Located near the Centro Cultural Banco do Brasil, this cultural center includes art exhibits, musical performances, and lectures relating to French and Brazilian culture.

❑ **Theatro Dulcina:** *Rua Alcindo Guanabara, 17 (Centro), Tel. 240-4879.* Opera and orchestra performances take place in the 600-seat theater.

❑ **Theatro João Caetano:** *Praça Tiradentes (Centro), Tel. 221-0305.* This 1,222-seat theater is the center for evening musical, dance, and comedic performances.

In addition to these major theaters and cultural centers, you'll find more than 65 other theaters throughout the city offering a variety of performances and exhibitions.

RIO CONNECTIONS

For more information on Rio de Janeiro, be sure to contact RIOTUR, the City of Rio de Janeiro Tourism Authority:

www.rio.rj.gov.br/riotur

This main website includes contact information on all RIOTUR offices worldwide.

In the United States, you can contact RIOTUR (also goes under the name of Myriad Travel Marketing) as follows:

RIOTUR
201 East 12th Street, Suite 509
New York, NY 10013
Tel. 212-375-0801
Fax 312-358-1263
Email: natalia@myriad.cc
Website: *www.destinationrio.com*

RIOTUR
3601 Aviation Boulevard, Suite 2100
Manhattan Beach, CA 90266
Tel. 310-643-2638
Fax 310-643-2627
Email: rio@myriad.cc
Website: *www.destinationrio.com*

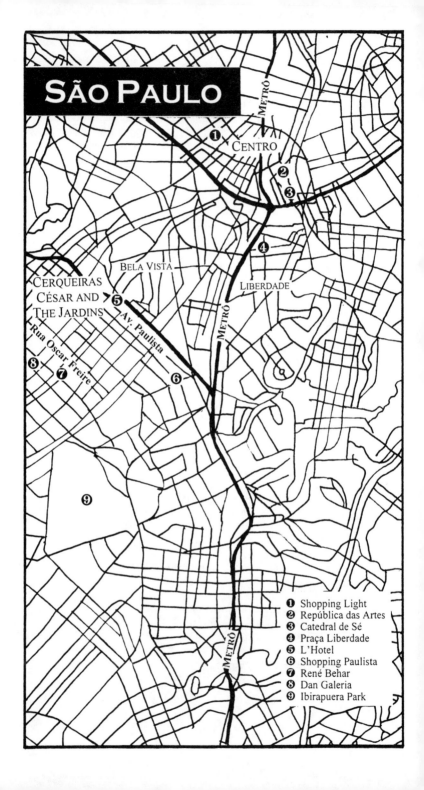

SÃO PAULO

CENTRO

METRÔ

BELA VISTA

LIBERDADE

CERQUEIRAS CÉSAR AND THE JARDINS

Av. Paulista

Rua Oscar Freire

METRÔ

METRÔ

❶ Shopping Light
❷ República das Artes
❸ Catedral de Sé
❹ Praça Liberdade
❺ L'Hotel
❻ Shopping Paulista
❼ René Behar
❽ Dan Galeria
❾ Ibirapuera Park

6

São Paulo

B RAZIL'S FINANCIAL AND MANUFACTURING powerhouse, São Paulo is both Brazil's and South America's largest city with nearly 20 million people. It begs comparison with its sunny rival, Rio de Janeiro. A very cosmopolitan city with a multi-ethnic population – including large Japanese, Italian, and Spanish-speaking minorities – São Paulo has a more international and business orientation than Rio. From its wide boulevards, skyscrapers, and traffic-choked streets to its chic international boutiques, antique shops, and restaurants, São Paulo has a more European feel to it than beachfront and festive Rio. While not as visually appealing as Rio, São Paulo has a great deal to offer visitors when it comes to quality shopping, dining, accommodations, sightseeing, and entertainment. Spend a few days here and you'll discover why the friendly locals love this sprawling metropolis. They, too, are the "beautiful people" but without beaches and mountains. São Paulo and its surrounding area has its own beat that makes it a very appealing place to visit.

A MELTING POT AND CITY OF HOPE

São Paulo is to Brazil what New York is to the United States – a great melting pot of many nationalities and cultures as well as a magnet for new economic opportunities. Indeed, São Paulo has a long history of attracting immigrants from all over the world who have helped build this city into a major economic center in South America. Starting near the end of the nineteenth century, immigrants from Europe and Asia came to São Paulo to build its coffee, textile, agricultural, and manufacturing industries. Today you'll see the vestiges of these early immigrants in the very cosmopolitan feel of the city, from architecture to restaurants. Visitors are often surprised to discover the largest Japanese immigrant community in the world (600,000 of Japanese heritage) resides in São Paulo, as well as encounter so many Italian, French, Portuguese, Spanish, Japanese, German, and restaurants. With over 1 million Italian immigrants settling in São Paulo state during the past century, this city has many good Italian restaurants. But the city also includes huge Lebanese (nearly 1 million), Spanish-speaking (1.5 million), German (100,000), and Eastern European (200,000 Russian, Armenian, and others) communities. Unlike Brazil's predominately Roman Catholic cities, at least one-third of São Paulo's population is non-Catholic, with Judaism, Shintoism, Buddhism, and Islam woven into its rich religious texture. If you are looking for the "real Brazil" in São Paulo, you won't find it in this uniquely structured city of international immigrants.

❑ São Paulo has a more international and business orientation than Rio.

❑ Like New York City, São Paulo is a great melting pot of many nationalities and cultures as well as a magnet for new economic opportunities.

❑ Each year nearly 300,000 people migrate to São Paulo in search of employment.

❑ This is a city of great wealth and sophistication, even though it is also home to a great deal of poverty and strained urban services.

In recent years São Paulo has also served as a magnet in attracting immigrants from all over Brazil who are drawn to factories in the huge industrial complex on the outskirts of the city. Nearly one-third of the population live in slums or tenements (cortiços). Indeed, in 1999 nearly 300,000 people migrated to São Paulo in search of employment, with many coming from the drought-stricken northeast, the region that disproportionately supplies labor to São Paulo and populates its many slums. From automobile and textile factories to chemical and steel plants, this is a working city that produces 45 percent of Brazil's industrial output (São Paulo state alone produces 65 percent). São Paulo's skyline of skyscrapers often shrouded in pollution testifies to its enormous manufacturing base, coupled with its role as the business and finance capital of Brazil. Its many shops, restaurants, and cultural venues are evidence that this is a city of great wealth and sophistication, even though it is also home to a great deal of poverty and strained urban services due to the constant influx of poor immigrants who see São Paulo as a city of economic hope, which indeed it is.

MEET MORE BEAUTIFUL PEOPLE

There's a certain smugness about this city that contrasts with the amusing narcissism of Rio. The friendly local residents of São Paulo, called the *paulistanos*, often view themselves as more serious and hard working than the more fun-loving, beach-obsessed *cariocas* of Rio. After all, the *paulistanos* are the economic backbone of the country. Indeed, many believe the country might collapse without their serious work ethic! Perhaps this attitude reflects a certain envy that the *cariocas* may be having too much fun at the expense of the *paulistanos*. At the same time, the *paulistanos* see themselves as the "beautiful people" who live in a modern sophisticated city of art, culture, and great shopping and chic dining opportunities. They love this huge city with its delightful multi-cultural and cosmopolitan environment. All you need to do is to go shopping and dining to understand their attitude toward this city of many surprises.

UNIQUE TREASURES AND PLEASURES

Unlike Rio, São Paulo lacks mountains, an ocean and beaches, and many old sites. Indeed, many visitors initially think this is only a city of big buildings designed for big businesses. Supporting this view is the fact that most visitors come to São Paulo on business rather than pleasure. As a result, São Paulo lacks the tourist infrastructure found in Rio. But there is lot more to this city than initial impressions. Especially for shoppers, this is a wonderful city – much better than more touristy Rio.

Like Rio, you can easily spend three to four days in and around São Paulo enjoying its many treasures and pleasures. And like Rio, there is something very seductive about this city. If you enjoy art, culture, and history, São Paulo will not disappoint you given its many museums, churches, theaters, and buildings. Shoppers have a wonderful time exploring São Paulo's many chic boutiques, art galleries, antique shops, markets, and shopping centers. And diners are rewarded with some of Brazil's best and trendiest restaurants. If you are a lifestyle shopper, you'll encounter the best of both worlds in São Paulo as you shop-and-dine 'til you drop! This is simply a great city for indulging your shopping and gastronomic fancies. And if you venture outside the city on weekends to such towns as Itu and Embu, you'll find even more delightful shopping and dining opportunities.

GETTING TO KNOW YOU

While you can find beautiful beaches within an hour's drive of São Paulo that rival those of Rio, São Paulo is essentially a flat and sprawling metropolis known for its many skyscrapers, apartment buildings, and unique neighborhoods that are home to Brazil's business elite. Indeed, this is a modern business city boasting numerous banks and factories as well as a few interesting historical and cultural sites. Much of the business of Brazil is done in the skyscrapers and restaurants that define downtown São Paulo.

❏ Unlike Rio, São Paulo lacks mountains, an ocean and beaches, and many old sites.

❏ Especially for shoppers, São Paulo is a wonderful city – much better than Rio.

❏ This is simply a great city for indulging your shopping and gastronomic fancies – the ultimate lifestyle shopping destination in Brazil.

❏ While you'll find several interesting buildings, plazas, monuments, churches, and museums in Centro, this area is not the best place for shopping or dining.

❏ Cerqueira César and the Jardins are the shopping and dining meccas of São Paulo.

Being such a large city, São Paulo can be quite intimidating to the first-time visitor. Once you arrive in São Paulo, be sure to pick up local literature on the city. Look for the *Hotel and Magazine Guide* (*Magazine Turismo & Hotelaria*), *São Paulo This Month*, and *São Paulo City Life*. These free magazines include English sections on everything from hotels and restaurants to sightseeing and entertainment. The first two publications also include useful maps of the city. If you enjoy shopping, sightseeing, and restaurants, you are well advised to stay in a central location, especially around Av. Paulista. For a real treat at a small boutique property, try L'Hotel São Paulo at Al. Campinas 266 in Jardim Paulista (Tel./Fax 283-0500) which is ideally located just off of Av. Paulista and between the sightseeing of Centro and the shopping of Jardim Paulista.

While São Paulo is large, most of your attention will probably be concentrated on three adjacent commercial areas which run north to southwest near the center of the city: Centro, Liberdades, and Cerqueira César. The latter area further extends into a few other popular commercial areas for upscale shopping and dining.

CENTRO

Centro is best known as downtown São Paulo because of its business activities, historical sites, and towering buildings. You can easily reach this area by taxi or Metrô (stops at Praça da Sé, São Bento, Anhangabaú, and Praça da Roosevelt). Encompassing the city's Lebanese and Syrian communities, Centro is one of the oldest sections of the city which is very mixed in terms of activities for visitors. If you enjoy quality shopping and dining, this is not the city's best destination. But sightseers especially enjoy visiting this busy section of the city. A pedestrian-friendly area with crowded streets, viaducts, and bridges, Centro is best covered on foot. Here you'll find several interesting buildings, plazas, parks, monuments, churches, and museums for spending a half to full day of sightseeing. Start at the main plaza, **Praça da Sé**, for exploring colonial São Paulo. This is the site of the huge neo-Gothic **Catedral Metropolitana**. As you explore the whole Centro area, you'll discover several interesting religious structures (**Pátio do Colégio**, **Igreja de São Francisco**, and **Santo Antônio**); colonial buildings (**Solar da Marquesa de Santos** and **Palácio das Indústrias**); museums (**Museu da Cidade**, **Museu de Arte Sacra**, and **Pinacoteca do Estado**); and city theater (**Teatro Municipal**). Many visitors ride to the top floors of skyscrapers to get panoramic views of the city – **Edifício Itália** (city's tallest building), **Edifício Sede do Banespa**, and **Edifício Martinelli** (city's first skyscraper). This area also includes the old municipal market (**Mercado Municipal**) which is located in the northeastern section of Centro (Rua Cantareira 306).

LIBERDADES

Located immediately south of Centro is the city's Japanese district, Liberdade. Easily reached by Metrô or a short walk from Praça da Sé in Centro, Liberdade is noted for its Japanese shops and restaurants (Rua Galvão Bueno), its **Feira Oriental** (Sunday Oriental Market, Praça da Liberdade, 10am - 7pm), and its museum, **Museu da Imigração Japonesa** (Rua São Joaquim, 381).

BELA VISTA (BIXIGA)

Located immediately to the west of Liberdades and southwest of Centro, Bela Vista (also called Bixiga) is São Paulo's "Little Italy." Here, you'll find a large concentration of Italian restaurants as well as an interesting museum documenting the history of this large Italian community, **Museu Memória do Bixga** (Rua dos Ingeleses, Wednesday to Sunday, 2-5:30pm).

CERQUEIRA CÉSAR AND THE JARDINS

Welcome to the best of the best in Brazil! Located southwest of Avenida Paulista, these two adjacent districts are São Paulo's shopping and dining meccas – and the best of the best lifestyle shopping areas in all of Brazil. This is where the "beautiful people" hang out in chic boutiques, top art galleries and antique shops, and trendy restaurants. Indeed, Jardim Paulista and Cerqueira César yield some of the best shopping in all of Brazil. The two and a half kilometer **Avenida Paulista** is to São Paulo what Fifth Avenue is to New York City, the symbol of a bustling commercial city lined with relatively nondescript buildings. Constructed in 1891 and initially lined with the mansions of Brazil's coffee barons, today this is a big and noisy commercial street with only one mansion remaining, the **House of Roses Museum** (Avenida Paulista, 37). Along this wide avenue you'll find numerous banks, office buildings, news-stands, the **Museu de Arte de São Paulo** (São Paulo Museum of Art), a surprisingly gorgeous McDonald's, the Shopping Paulista mall, and a few interesting weekend markets. But the really "good stuff" in this area lies a few blocks west and southwest of the avenue and especially along **Rua Oscar Freire** and its adjacent upscale shopping and dining streets – Al. Casa Branca, Al. Lorena, R. Peixoto Gomide, Al. Ministro Rocha Azevedo, R. Padre João Manuel, R. Haddock Lobo, R. Bela Cintra, Al. Franca, and R. Estados Unidos. This is a great lifestyle shopping area with many trendy shops and restaurants exuding lots of ambience. The best strategy is to begin at the southwest end of Rua Oscar Freire, beginning near the intersection with Al. Casa Branca, and walk northwest until you come to the end which is at Rua da Consalaçã – a long and shop-filled journey. Walking this area yields many exciting discoveries. Here you'll find São Paulo's top clothing, jewelry, art, antique, and home decorative shops as well as designer boutiques. Spend a day or two in this area and you'll come away with a very different view of São Paulo and Brazil – a place of top quality shopping and dining. Farther west of this upscale shopping and dining area are two adjacent museums, Museu da Imagem e do Som (Avenida Europa, 158) and Museu Brasiliero de Escultura (Avenida Europa, 218).

SHOPPING SÃO PAULO

Shopping is one of São Paulo's major attractions. After all, this is a business and convention city that attracts many upscale international travelers who seek out the best of the best in this vibrant city. Being more cosmopolitan than Rio, São Paulo has the feel of an international city.

The city's major shopping strengths include clothes – especially imported and local designer labels – art, antiques, jewelry, handicrafts, and home decorative items. Many of the shops here are simply outstanding, reflecting a level of quality not found elsewhere in Brazil.

The best shopping in this city tends to be concentrated in two adjacent areas just southwest of Avenida Paulista – Jardim Paulista and Cerqueira César. Shops in this area also extend farther west into two other adjacent districts – Jardim América and Pinheiros. Within these areas, Rua Oscar Freire is the center of the shopping action. Indeed, if you have limited time in São Paulo, you are well advised to head for this area of the city for all your shopping and dining needs. You won't be disappointed – only exhausted after a hard day of shopping and dining!

❑ The city's major shopping strengths include clothes, arts, antiques, jewelry, handicrafts, and home decorative items.

❑ São Paulo's most popular weekend markets are open on Sunday from 10am to 5-6pm.

❑ Since this city is a major center for design, art, and antiques, expect to find trendy boutiques of major local designers, high-end antique shops, top art galleries, and unique home decorative and handicraft shops.

❑ Unlike Rio's antique shops, which have more Brazilian content, São Paulo's antique shops tend to be more upscale and international.

Like Rio, São Paulo has its share of weekend markets which usually operate on Sunday. Most shops are open during weekdays (9am - 6pm) and part of Saturday (9am to 1pm or 2pm); most close on Sundays. Large shopping centers are open Monday through Saturday, 10am - 10pm, and on Sunday afternoon. Hours of weekend markets vary, depending on the particular market. The most popular markets are open on Sunday, 10am - 5pm. It's always good to check with your hotel concerning the operating hours of different markets.

WHAT TO BUY

Shoppers in São Paulo discover a wide range of local and imported products that reflect the interests and buying habits of its clientele. Since this city attracts many business people and convention groups and has many affluent and cosmopolitan locals, São Paulo tends to have many shops of interest to individuals in search of unique, quality items. Since this city is a major center for design, art, and antiques, expect to find trendy boutiques of major local designers, high-end antique shops, top art galleries, and unique home decorative and handicraft shops. Here's what you are likely to find in São Paulo:

❑ **Gemstones and jewelry:** Similar to what you will find in Rio, the highly competitive H. Stern and Amsterdam Sauer are major players in São Paulo's gemstone and jewelry trade. You'll find **H. Stern** shops at the international airport and throughout the city in the major shopping districts (Praça da Repúblic, 242; R. Augusta 2340; R. Oscar Freire, 652); six shopping centers, including Iguatemi, Ibirapuera, Morumbi, and Paulista; and 15 hotels, including L'Hotel, Inter-Continental, Maksoud Plaza, Hilton, and Sheraton). **Amsterdam Sauer** also has shops at the international airport; A. São Luis, 29; shopping centers (Iguatemi and Morumbi); and hotels (Maksoud Plaza and Sheraton). You'll find many other shops offering good quality jewelry and gemstones in the Centro, Liberdade, and Jardim Paulista districts (**Reisman**, Rua Barão de Itapetininga, 50, Centro, Tel. 255-1401, website: *www.reisman.com.br*; **Santa Gema**, R. Oscar Freire, 691, Tel. 881-1533; **Natan**, R. Oscar Freire, 672, Tel. 280-2233; and Antônio Bernardo, Rua Bela Cintra, 2063, Tel. 883-5034) as well as great Italian costume jewelry (**Edna D'Bezerra**, Rua Oscar Freire, 583, Tel. 3063-2949). Both cut and uncut precious Brazilian stones can be found at the popular Sunday market (9am - 4pm) near Praça da República in Centro.

❑ **Art and art galleries:** If you love art, it doesn't get much better than what you find in São Paulo. Indeed, the best art tends to find its way into São Paulo's best galleries and shops. Some of Brazil's top art is well represented in São Paulo's many fine art galleries, which tend to be disproportionately found in the adjacent Cerqueira César and the Jardins areas. For paintings of Brazilian modern masters, as well as top contemporary Brazilian artists, be sure to visit **Dan Galeria** (Rua Estados Unidos, 1638, Tel. 883-4600, website: *www.dangaleria.com.br*). Other excellent art galleries includes **Renot** (Al. Min. Rocha Azevedo, 1327, Tel. 883-5933); **Casa Triângulo** (R. Bento Freitas, 33, Centro, Tel. 220-5910); **Gabinette de Arte Raquel Arnaud** (R. Artur

Azevedo, 401, Pinheiros, Tel. 883-6322); **Luísa Strina** (R.
Pe. João Manuel, 974-A, Tel. 280-2471); and **Ena Beçak**
(R. Oscar Freire, 440, Tel. 280-7322, website: *www.enabecak.
com.br*) which also includes a restaurant/cafe. For stone and
bronze sculptures, be sure to visit the expansive **Skultura**
(R. Bela Cintra, 2023, Tel. 280-5911). For primitive or *arte
naïf*, visit **Galeria Jacques Ardies** (R. Do Livramento, 221,
Pq. Ibirapuera, Tel. 884-2916). For contemporary ceramics,
engravings, drawings, and paintings, visit **Toki Arte e
Objetos** (R. Itápolis, 287, Pacaembu, Tel. 826-6091).

❑ **Antiques, home decorative items, and antiquities:** São
Paulo is an antique lover's paradise that can keep you busy
for a few days of "antiquing." Unlike Rio's antique shops,
which have more Brazilian content, with lots of furniture
and small collectibles, São Paulo's antique shops tend to be
more upscale and international in orientation. Numerous
shops offer high-end European as well as Brazilian antiques.
Popular with designers, some of these shops function more
as home decorative shops than strictly antique shops. Many
of these shops are concentrated in the upscale Cerqueira
César and Jardim Paulista shopping areas as well as extend
west into adjacent Jardim América and Pinheiros areas. For
wonderful home decorative items, which include tasteful
selections of antiques and furniture in a beautiful setting, be
sure to visit **Renée Behar** (R. Peixoto Gomide, 2088, Tel.
853-3622, website: *www.reneebehar.com.br*) as well as her
nearby warehouse-shop, **84 Antiguidades** (R. Prof. Azevedo Amaral, 84, Tel. 883-7880). Some of the best antique
dealers, all located in Jardim Paulista and Cerqueira César
areas, include: **Edoardo E Ariane Juliani L'antiguário** (R.
Padre João Manuel, 1050, Tel. 280-2625); **Tony Antiguidades** (Rua Estados Unidos, 1470, Tel. 852-8488);
Nóbrega Antiquario & Galeria de Arte (R. Padre João
Manuel, 1231, Tel. 3068-9388); and **Country House
Antiques** (R. Padre João Manuel, 1242, Tel. 3064-2119).
For a unique collection of ethnic arts and antiques from
Brazil and Southeast Asia, be sure to visit Christian-Jack
Heymès at his wonderful small shop, **Patrimonio/AOA** (Al.
Ministro Rocha Azevedo, 1068, Tel. 3064-1750). A few
shops offer antiquities from Central and South America.
The best such shop is **Marcelo de Medeiros** (Rua Francisco
Dias Velhi, 203, Brooklin, Tel. 5561-0083, by appointment
only) with its fabulous collection of Indian antiquities and
local religious art.

❑ **Clothes and fabrics:** Most of Brazil's major designers are well represented in São Paulo's many boutiques. Several boutiques also represent imported European and U.S. fashion. Most of these shops are located along or near Rua Oscar Freire in Jardim Paulista and Cerqueira César. We especially like **Eclat** (Rua Peixoto Gomide, 2067, Tel. 3086-1515; also at Shopping Center Iguatemi, Tel. 816-6493) with its many international lines of fashionable clothes and local accessories. Also look for **Daslu** (R. Domingos Lerne, 284, Tel. 822-3785); **Forum** (Rua Oscar Freire, 916, Tel. 853-6269); and **Viva Vida** (Rua Oscar Freire, 969, Tel. 280-0421). For fashionable children's clothes, visit **Dulce** (Rua Oscar Freire, 673, Tel. 282-4956). If you are interested in both local and imported fabrics, visit **Firenze** (Rua Augusta, 2781, Tel. 280-2022, website: *www.firenzetecidos. com.br*) for Brazilian cotton, silk, and wool as well as fabrics from Italy, Japan, France, and England.

❑ **Tribal arts and crafts:** São Paulo has a few excellent shops which offer good collections of Indian arts and crafts from throughout Brazil. Our favorite shop, which is also reputed to be the best in São Paulo, is **Casa do Amazonas** (Al. Dos Jurupis, 460, Moema, Tel. 5051-3098), a combination museum and artifact shop. **Amoa Konoya** (Rua Joāno Moura, 1002, Jardim América, Tel. 3061-0639), a small and cramped shop, offers some interesting Indian artifacts. Visit both shops and you will be exposed to a good range of quality Indian arts and crafts.

❑ **Handicrafts:** São Paulo also is a major center for arts and crafts from all over the country. Look for lace from the northeast, carved wooden saints, masks, primitive paintings, fashion jewelry, batiks, hammocks, bowls, porcelain dolls, and T-shirts. For local handicrafts, visit **Galeria de Arte Brasileira** (2163 Alameda Lorena, Tel. 852-9452); **SUTA-CO** (Praça da República Metrô station and Avenue Angélica, 2582, Tel. 231-2404); **Ana** (Arts Nativa Aplicada, Rua Melo Alves, 184, Tel. 282-3559); **Arte-India** (FUNAI, Rua Augusta, 1371, Tel. 283-2102); **O Bode** (Rua Bela Cintra, 2009); **Kabuletê** (Rua Dr Melo Alves); and **Transas Brasileiras** (Av. Paulista, 2001, Tel. 287-2016). The weekend markets, especially along Av. Paulista (at the São Paulo Museum of Art and across the street at the park), are filled with stalls offering a wide range of handicrafts.

WHERE TO SHOP

While São Paulo is a huge, sprawling city, its shopping is confined to a few well-defined areas, department stores, and markets. In many respects, this is a very easy city to shop once you understand where everything can be found on a map.

SHOPPING AREAS AND STREETS

São Paulo basically has two major shopping areas, Centro and an area just southwest of Avenida Paulista, which are easy to get to and require a great deal of walking. These areas have the highest concentration of similar quality and product shops. A few top quality shops are scattered in other areas throughout the city.

CENTRO

This highly concentrated and often pedestrian-friendly central business district is known for its tall buildings and historical sites. It also has many shops, from clothing and accessories to jewelry and art, that primarily cater to local shoppers. While you'll find lots of clothes and shoes in this area, don't expect to see designer goods or even the latest in fashion. The major shopping streets here are located immediately to the northwest and southeast of Praça da República; most connect in the southeast to Avenida Ipiranga – Rua 24 de Maio, Rua Barão de Itapetinga, Rua do Arouche, and Rua Dom José de Barros. You'll also find many street vendors crowding the sidewalks in this area. **Rua do Arouche** is known for its many shops offering leather shoes, bags, and accessories. Many shops along **Ruas Sete de Abril, Barão de Itapetininga**, and **24 de Maio** specialize in precious and semi-precious gemstones, handicrafts, and souvenirs. **Rua 25 de Março** is popular with visitors from other Brazilian cities who come here to buy fabrics, accessories, toys, and assorted items as well as visit the many restaurants and snack bars that line this street. One street has nearly 100 shops specializing in bridal gowns and wedding clothes – **Rua São Caetano**, opposite Luz Park.

We find Centro to be more of a cultural experience than an adventure in quality shopping. Check it out when you're sightseeing in this area but don't make a special trip here for shopping in expectation of finding top quality goods. The most interesting shopping in this area may be at the Sunday outdoor bazaar (9am - 4pm), located near Praça da República (replaces the old Sunday Hippie Fair which used to be held at Praça da República): **República das Artes** (Av. Ipiranga, between Avenida São Luís and Rua da Consolação). This market includes lots of Brazilian cut and uncut precious stones, stamps, lace, souvenirs, woodcarvings, leather goods, paintings, ceramics, and handicrafts.

CERQUEIRAS CÉSAR AND THE JARDINS

The really good shopping in São Paulo is found along several major shopping streets in the upscale suburbs of Cerqueira César and the Jardins (Jardim Paulista, Jardim América, Pinheiros) that lie to the southwest of Avenida Paulista. Known as Brazil's "Manhattan" and "5th Avenue," here's where you will find the city's largest concentration of upscale boutiques, art galleries, antique and home decorative shops, and clothing and accessory stores. Encompassing dozens of blocks, this rectangular shopping district is bounded by Al Casa Branca on the southeast, R. Estabos Unidos on the southwest, R. da Consolação on the northwest, and José Maria Lisboa on the northeast. The main shopping street, running from the southeast (starting at the intersection of Al Casa Branca) to the northwest (ending at R. da Comsolação) is **Rua Oscar Freire**. We prefer starting at the southeast end of the street and walking northwest. Along the way, you should explore several intersecting streets, especially Al. Lorena, R. Peixoto Gomide, R. Prof. Azevedo Amaral, Al. Ministro Rocha Azevedo, R. Padre João Manuel, R. Augusta, R. Haddock Loba, and R. Bela Cintra. In fact, many of this area's most interesting shops are found on these adjacent and nearby streets. Since this is a truly a lifestyle shopping area, with several excellent cafes and restaurants along the way, plan to spend a day or two in this delightful area doing what many locals and visitors love to do together – shop and dine. Some of our favorite streets and shops in this area include:

❑ **Rua Oscar Freire:** This street is lined with numerous shops. It's best approached by just walking the whole street and stopping at shops that appeal to your interests and tastes. **Edna D'Bezerra** (#583, Tel. 3063-2949) for a very fashionable collection of Italian costume jewelry and sunglasses; **Natan** (#672, Tel. 280-2233) for exclusive jewelry, porcelain, crystal, and accessories; **Forum** (#916, Tel. 853-6269) for fashions by designer Tufi Duek; **Movimiento Natural** (#1035) for cotton lingerie; **Rosa Cha** (#977, Tel. 881-2793) for colorful beachwear; **José Carlos Couture** (#600, Tel. 853-7668) for fashionable clothes; **Ena Beçak** (#440,

Tel. 280-7322) for paintings in a café setting; **Myriam Barbosa Mello Antiques** (#232, casa 8, Tel. 852-6934) for a very cluttered collection of furniture, ceramics, lamps, silver, rugs, carvings, and collectibles; **Dulce** (#673, Tel. 282-4956) for a nice collection of children's clothes, including smocked dresses. Also, look for such name brand shops as **La Coste, Mont Blanc, Polo Ralph Lauren, Victor Hugo, Tommy Hilfiger, Baccarat, Bally,** and **Lalique**.

❑ **Rua Peixoto Gomide:** A "must visit" shop here is **Renée Behar** (#2088, Tel. 853-3622) with its excellent collection of antiques, furniture and home decorative items in a lovely setting; **Eclat** (#2067, Tel. 3086-1515) for beautiful clothes and accessories; and **British Home** (#1789, Tel. 853-4127) for two shops filled with quality carpets, furniture, ceramics, silver, and collectibles.

❑ **Rua Estados Unidos:** There's not much here except for two of the city's top art and antique shops. Visit **Dan Galeria** (#1638, Tel. 883-4600) for an excellent collection of paintings by Brazilian masters and contemporary artists; and **Tony Antiquidades** (#1470, Tel. 852-8488) for high-end French antiques.

❑ **Rua Padre João Manuel:** This street includes some exceptional quality antique shops. Be sure to visit **Edoardo E Ariane Juliani** (#1050, Tel. 852-3860) for two floors of top quality antique and decorative items; **Nóbrega Antiquario & Galeria de Arte** (#1231, Tel. 3068-9388) for an excellent collection of Brazilian, European, and Asian antiques; and **Country House Antiques** (#1242, Tel. 3064-2119) for lots of furniture, porcelain, and bronze.

❑ **Alameda Lorena:** This street is filled with interesting discoveries. Visit **Artes Steiner** (#1909, Tel. 280-3555) for a good collection of paintings and sculptures produced by modern Brazilian artists; **Tappeti Antichi** (#1263, Tel. 280-3310) for a nice selection of old and new Persian rugs; **Jan Schultz Antiquário** (#881, Tel. 280-2174) for two floors of tasteful antiques and paintings; **Antonio Carlos Brito** (#889, Tel. 280-8696) for furniture, rugs, and an occasional collectible; and **Galeria de Arts Brasileira** (#2163, Tel. 852-9452) for Brazilian arts and crafts, including primitive paintings.

❑ **Rua Haddock Lobo:** This street includes several name brand shops such as **Mont Blanc, Louis Vuitton, Cartier,** and **Godiva**.

❑ **Rua Augusta:** This busy street includes numerous shops of varying quality. Check out **Firenze** (#2781, Tel. 280-2022) for both Brazilian and imported fabrics; **H. Stern** (#2340, Tel. 256-6057) for fashionable jewelry and gemstones; and **Park Pedras** (#1523, Tel. 288-0819) for Brazilian stones and jewelry.

❑ **Al. Ministro Rocha Azevedo:** Two of our favorite galleries are found here. Visit **Renot** (#1327, Tel. 883-5933) for a wide range of Brazilian paintings and tapestries (upstairs); and **Patrimonio/AOA** (#1068, Tel. 3064-1750) for a unique collection of South American Indian and Southeast Asian arts, crafts, and artifacts.

❑ **Rua Bela Cintra:** This is the northeast border street in this shopping area. Look for **Antonio Bernardo** (#2063, Tel. 883-5622) for unique modern jewelry in an understated setting; and **Skultura** (#2023, Tel. 280-5911) for a wide selection of sculptures, most of which are cast in bronze and unsigned. Also, look for name-brand shops such as **Godiva, Kenzo,** and **Emporio Armani**.

OTHER DISCOVERIES

A few excellent quality shops are spread throughout the city in various neighborhoods. You'll most likely need to take taxis to find these places, which are well worth the extra effort and cost of transportation. For example, **Marcelo de Medeiros**, which is one of Brazil's top Indian antiquity and religious art shops, is operated from the owner's large residential complex in Brooklin district (Rua Francisco Dias Velho, 203, Tel. 5561-0083, by appointment only). Just northeast of Brooklin, in the district of Moema, you'll find one of the city's best Indian arts and crafts shops, **Casa do Amazonas** (Al. Dos Jurupis, 460, Tel. 5051-3098). On weekends you may want to rent a car to explore the delightful colonial town of **Itu** and the arts and crafts town of **Embu**. Both towns are within a one-hour drive of São Paulo.

SHOPPING CENTERS

São Paulo has more than 20 shopping centers which are especially popular with local residents. Offering a wide range of shopping options, many of these palatial centers include fountains, mirrored walls, cinemas, food courts, and playgrounds. Most of these places are open Monday through Saturday, 10am - 10pm, although some open at 9am on Saturday. The city's six major shopping centers include:

❑ **Shopping Light:** *Rua Xavier de Toledo and Viaduto do Chá, (Centro).* The city's newest and classiest shopping center located across the street from the Municipal Theater. Includes many upscale shops, especially fashion boutiques and interior design shops, as well as a good selection of cafes and restaurants.

❑ **D&D Decoração & Design Center:** *Av. Das Naïções Unidas, 12551 (Brooklin Novo), Tel. 3043-9000.* Attached to the World Trade Center and the Gran Meliá Hotel, this center includes 120 stores with 80 being decorator shops.

❑ **Morumbi:** *Av. Roque Petroni Jr., 1089 (Morumbi), Tel. 533-2444.* One of São Paulo's most upscale shopping centers with many major boutiques and designer shops represented.

❑ **Iguatemi:** *Av. Brig. Faria Lima, 2232 (Pinheiros), Tel. 816-6116.* One of the city's oldest and most elegant shopping centers that remains very popular with local shoppers.

❑ **Eldorado:** *Av. Rebouças, 3970 (Pinheiros), Tel. 870-0688.* The largest and most diverse shopping center with fountains and lots of glass. Not particularly upscale.

❑ **Shopping Paulista:** *R. Treze de Maio, 1947 (Paulista), Tel. 253-8166.* Includes numerous boutiques and fast food restaurants.

MARKETS

São Paulo also has its share of markets. Most are open on Sunday but some are open during the week. If you plan to visit these markets, you may want to carefully schedule your Sunday because the city markets also compete with the popular arts and crafts market in Embu, a town located 27 kilometers west of São Paulo (see the section on Embu at the very end of this chapter). The city's most popular markets include:

❑ **Antiquidades do MASP:** *Museu de Arte de São Paulo (MASP), Av. Paulista, 1578. Open Sunday, 10am - 5pm.* This

well organized antique and collectible market includes over
100 dealer stalls which are set up under the open area of the
São Paulo Musuem of Art. Includes everything from army
helmets, old trains, and cameras to china, glass, jewelry,
watches, silver, toys, books, and bronzes. Includes some
Indian crafts and religious figures. Across the street, in front
of the Parque Tenente Siqueria Campos, is a sidewalk bazaar
with numerous vendors offering a wide range of handicrafts,
leather goods, clothes, jewelry, paintings, and food. Talented
sidewalk musicians entertain as well as sell CDs of their
recordings.

❑ **República das Artes:** *Ave. Ipiranga (Centro). Open Sunday,
9am - 4pm.* Located near Praça da República and in front of
the Hilton São Paulo Hotel (between Avenida São Luis and
Rua da Consolação), this popular weekend market offers
many both cut and uncut gemstones, woodcarvings, leather
goods, toys, clothing, handmade lace, stamps, ceramics, and
souvenirs. Look for street artists displaying their paintings on
the side streets leading to the park (praça). This outdoor
bazaar replaces the old Sunday Hippie Fair which used to be
held in the park.

❑ **Mercado Municipal:** *Rua da Cantareira, 306 (Centro). Open
Monday to Sunday, 5am - 4pm.* If you're interesting in seeing
a large fresh market of fruits, vegetables, and fish, this is the
ultimate place to visit. One of the best such markets in Brazil.

❑ **Feira Oriental:** *Praça da Liberdade (Liberdade). Open Sunday,
10am - 7pm.* Located in the Japanese district, this market
includes gemstones, handicrafts, plants, and food.

❑ **Antiquidades e Artes:** *Praça Benedito Calixto (Pinheiros). Open
Saturday and Sunday, 9am - 6pm.* This large bazaar includes
lots of bric-a-brac and collectibles as well as several
restaurants and food stalls.

❑ **Mercado de Flores:** *Largo de Arouche (Centro).* This popular
flower market is open daily.

BEST OF THE BEST

If you have limited time for shopping in São Paulo, you may
want to focus on the following shops. We found these shops to
be of exceptional quality or of particular note because of their

unique offerings and service. Visiting these shops will put you in
touch with some of the best shopping in São Paulo.

GEMS AND JEWELRY

❑ **Antonoi Bernardo:** *Rua Bela Cintra, 2063 (Cerqueira César/
Jardins), Tel. 883-5622; and Shopping Iguatemi, Av. Brigadeiro
Faria Lima, 1191, LJ. P5, Tel. 816-3777.* Don't let this
understated, minimalist shop dissuade you from exploring is
fine work. Its talented designer produces beautiful modern
and classic silver and gold jewelry. Many of the pieces are
designed with precious stones.

❑ **H. Stern:** *Rua Augusta, 2340 (Cerqueira César/Jardins), Tel.
256-6057, and Praça da Repúblic, 242. Also has small shops at
the International Airport, six major shopping centers, and 15 major
hotels.* Represents Brazil's largest and most famous gem and
jewelry dealer. Beautiful jewelry designs. Difficult to miss
since H. Stern is so ubiquitous throughout the city's major
shopping centers and hotels.

❑ **Edna D'Bezerra:** *Rua Oscar Freire, 583 (Cerqueira César/
Jardins), Tel. 3063-2949.* This is a fun shop for great-looking
costume jewelry, sunglasses, watches, hair pins, and purses.
Most items are imported from Italy. Look for excellent copies
of Cartier jewelry.

ART

❑ **Dan Galeria:** *Rua Estados Unidos, 1638 (Cerqueira César/
Jardins), Tel. 883-4600. Website: **www.dangaleria.com.br**.* One
of Brazil's very best art galleries. Represents 18 of Brazil's top
contemporary artists. Includes many master artists. Has an
international presence in Europe and North America.
Regularly hosts shows and includes catalogs of collections.
Very expensive – for serious collectors only.

❑ **Renot:** *Al. Ministro Rocha Azevedo (Cerqueira César/Jardins),
1327, Tel. 883-5933.* This two-story gallery represents more
than 30 Brazilian artists, many of whom are major artists.
Regularly hosts shows. Tapestries upstairs are made by the
owner, Renot. Includes religious and African antiques among
its many paintings. Catalogs available.

❑ **Skultura:** *Rua Bela Cintra, 2023, Tel. 280-5911 (Cerqueira
César/Jardins).* If you're in the market for bronze sculptures

and related works of art, be sure to visit this expansive two-story gallery. Represents nearly 40 artists who produce some very attractive sculptures. Most are cast in bronze. However, while some are signed by the sculptor, none are both signed and numbered, which tends to diminish their value. While we like this attractive gallery, many pieces may seem overpriced since they are not both signed and numbered.

❑ **Ena Beçak:** *Rua Oscar Freire, 440 (Cerqueira César/Jardins), Tel. 280-7322. Website:* ***www.enabecak.com.br****. Open Monday to Friday, 9:30am - 7:30pm, and Saturday, 9:30am - 4:30pm.* The modern architectural style (think Soho in New York City) of this combination art gallery, events center, gift shop, and café (serves breakfast, lunch, and snacks) has a very inviting and trendy look to it. Collectively known as **Ena Beçak**, this place actually comes under three names: **Espaço Cultural Ena Beçak**, **Choice Art Gallery**, and **Café Bistrot**. It's a center for art exhibits and special events. Exhibits, which include paintings (primarily Brazilian artists), sculptures, glassware, and ceramics, are found on both the first and second floors. The exhibits change monthly. Includes four special exhibits each year. Check out their interesting website for further information, including upcoming exhibits and special events during your stay in São Paulo.

ANTIQUES, HOME DECORATIVE ITEMS, AND ANTIQUITIES

❑ **René Behar:** *R. Peixoto Gomide, 2088 (Cerqueira César/Jardins), Tel. 853-3622 or Fax 853-9338. Website:* ***www.reneebehar.com. br****. Also has a warehouse called 84 Antiguidades at R. Prof. Azevedo Amaral, 84, Tel. 883-7880.* One of the nicest antique and home decorative shops in Brazil, a real classy operation. Especially popular with designers and decorators. Housed in a lovely old house with an English conservatory/gazebo attached. Includes two floors of quality paintings, tapestries, furniture, rugs, and accessories, with lots of blue and white items. The owner and interior decorator, René, also displays her extensive collection of Napolean memorabilia as well as her own bottled fragrance which is similar to Calvin Klein's creation. Includes a gift department at the back of the shop. Changing window displays and selections give this shop a real designer touch.

❑ **Marcelo de Medeiros:** *Rua Francisco Dias Velhi, 203 (Brooklin), Tel. 5561-0083, Fax 531-5882. By appointment only.*

Here's a real collector's find. Housed in the owner's residential compound, this private home and gallery is jam-packed with a combination of religious art and antiques and Indian antiquities from Brazil and Peru. The shop in the rear of the compound is primarily devoted to religious art, much of which is from the colonial period: religious figures, statuary, icons, altars, pots, paintings, furniture, and chests. The upstairs shop, near the front of the compound, houses the owner's extensive collection of excavated pre-Columbian antiquities which are displayed on numerous racks of shelves. Includes beautiful works of art, especially pottery and a few textiles. Also has a private collection in his adjacent house which he shows to some visitors upon request. Not set up to take credit cards but may take personal checks. Does excellent packing and shipping. If you're looking for top quality religious art and pre-Columbian antiquities, it doesn't get better than this fine shop.

❑ **Edoardo E Ariane Juliani L'antiguário:** *Rua Padre João Manuel, 1050 (Cerqueira César/Jardins), Tel. 280-2625.* Popular with serious antique collectors, designers, and decorators alike, this antique shop includes a top quality collection of fine antiques from both Brazil and Europe – paintings, furniture, lamps, rugs, and unusual pieces. Includes three rooms on the first floor and an upstairs area.

❑ **Tony Antiguidades:** *Rua Estados Unidos, 1470 (Cerqueira César/Jardins), Tel. 852-8488.* You'll think you're in France as soon as you step into this palatial two-story shop of French antique furniture, bronze sculptures, and chandeliers (terrific collection). The upstairs area also includes some English, Dutch, and German antiques. Restoration room at the back of the shop is usually busy working on new acquisitions. Very expensive and very exclusive. Definitely a place for high-end antique collectors. Boasts an international clientele that has been shopping here for more than 25 years.

❑ **Nóbrega Antiquario & Galeria de Arte:** *Rua Padre João Manuel, 1231 (Cerqueira César/Jardins), Tel. 3068-9388.* Offers a wonderful collection of quality paintings, tapestries, furniture, rugs, silver, and sculptures in an inviting gallery setting. Includes some religious and Asian art. A well established shop in São Paulo for more than 60 years.

❑ **Patrimonio/AOA:** *Al. Ministro Rocha Azevedo, 1068 (Cerqueira César/Jardins), Tel. 3064-1750.* This somewhat unusual and eclectic two-story gallery/shop includes a unique combination of Brazilian and Southeast Asian (primarily from Borneo) ethnic arts and antiques which appeal to wide range of visitors, from serious collectors to tourists in search of quality handcrafted items to take back home and display as a memento of their trip to Brazil. Most items are small collectibles – carvings, feather pieces, and ceramics – although the shop includes some Brazilian furniture. Frenchman Christian-Jack Heymès, who has made Brazil his home for more than 15 years, has an artist's and designer's eye and enthusiasm for collecting some truly outstanding pieces and then mounting and displaying them well. He knows the stories behind each piece and is happy to share his extensive knowledge with visitors. Christian-Jack also designs his own pieces. Includes a very nice collection of tribal feather pieces used in rituals. Be sure to visit the upstairs area which includes many interesting tribal pieces.

CLOTHES

❑ **Eclat:** *Rua Peixoto Gomide, 2067 (Cerqueira César/Jardins), Tel. 3086-1515; also at Shopping Center Iguatemi, Tel. 816-6493.* Located directly across the street from René Behar, this elegant boutique and showroom offers very fashionable designer label clothes from Europe and the United States. Includes small fashionable handbags produced by Glorinha Paranaguá in Rio. Also includes Pashmina scarves and fashionable shoes and leather coats.

❑ **Daslu:** *Rua Domingos Lerne, 284 (Vila Nova Conceição), Tel. 822-3785.* This exclusive boutique includes Daslu's own line along with designer clothes by Karl Lagerfeld and Chanel.

❑ **Forum:** *Rua Oscar Freire, 916 (Cerqueira César/Jardins), Tel. 853-6269.* This is the main shop of noted Brazilian designer Tufi Duek. Includes many trendy designs.

❑ **Dulce:** *Rua Oscar Freire, 673 (Cerqueira César/Jardins), Tel. 282-4956.* Includes a nice collection of children's clothing, especially attractive smocked dresses.

❑ **Firenze:** *Rua Augusta, 2781, Tel. 280-2022 (Cerqueira César/ Jardins). Website: www.firenzetecidos.com.br.* This popular traditional fabric shop (sold by the meter) includes a wide selection of Brazilian cotton, silk, and wool fabrics along with imported fabrics from Italy, Japan, France, and England.

TRIBAL ARTS AND CRAFTS

❑ **Casa do Amazonas:** *Al. Dos Jurupis, 460 (Moema), Tel. 5051-3098.* This shop represents the artifacts and ritual art of several of the more than 70 Indian tribes that primarily live in the interior of Brazil. The really nice things are found upstairs. However, this area is roped off as the owner's museum. Go upstairs to take a look, but don't fall in love with anything because you won't be able to buy it. The downstairs and staircase have a wide selection of good quality Indian arts and crafts, from masks, baskets, and woodcarvings to feathered headdresses, hammocks, weapons, ceramics, stools, pots, gourds, and belts. No English spoken here – only Japanese and Portuguese – but sign language works well.

❑ **Amoa Konoya:** *Rua Joāno Moura, 1002 (Jardim América), Tel. 3061-0639.* This very small tribal arts and crafts shop is jam-packed with pots, carvings, headdresses, baskets, masks, stools, beads, weapons, gourds, books, and CDs from various Brazilian tribes. The owner/collector enthusiastically explains individual items in the collection. Since this shop is off the popular shopping paths, it's best to take a taxi here and then have the shop call for a taxi when you leave.

❑ **Arte-India:** *FUNAI, Rua Augusta, 1371 (Cerqueira César/Jardins), Tel. 283-2102.* Includes numerous arts and crafts produced by various Indian tribes in Brazil. A government-operated shop.

❑ **Patrimonio/AOA:** *Al. Ministro Rocha Azevedo, 1068 (Cerqueira César/Jardins), Tel. 3064-1750.* See above entry under our "Antiques, Home Decorative Items, and Antiquities" section.

HANDICRAFTS

❑ **Galeria de Arte Brasileira:** *2163 Alameda Lorena, (Cerqueira César/Jardins), Tel. 852-9452.* If you're looking for gifts and souvenirs, this place has lots to choose from – carved bowls, masks, animals, and wooden saints; hammocks; primitive paintings and popular art; Brazilian stones and jewelry; Indian crafts; batiks; lace; and T-shirts.

❑ **SUTACO:** *Praça da República Metrô station (Centro), Tel. 257-4386,. and Avenida Angélica, 2582 (near Avenida Paulista), Tel. 231-2404.* This organization and shop promotes numerous handicrafts produced in the state of São Paulo.

❑ **Ana:** *Arts Nativa Aplicada, Rua Dr. Melo Alves, 184 (Cerqueira César/Jardins), Tel. 282-3559.* Includes cotton and wool fabrics printed with attractive Brazilian tribal designs. Offers a small collection of ceramics.

❑ **Weekend markets:** Be sure to check out a few of the major weekend markets (mainly on Sunday) which have a large collection of handcrafted items. You may find some excellent quality treasures amongst the mediocre offerings. See our entries above, under the "Market" section, for **Antiquidades do MASP** (especially the vendors operating in front of the park across the street) and **República das Artes**. Also, check out the shops and markets in the nearby arts and crafts towns of **Itu** and **Embu** (see entries below).

ACCOMMODATIONS

As a major business city, São Paulo has several excellent quality four- and five-star hotels centrally located near the major business districts of Centro and Avenida Paulista. The city's best hotels include:

❑ **L'Hotel São Paulo:** *Alameda Campinas 266, São Paulo, SP, 01404-000, Brazil, Tel. (55 11) 283-0500, Fax (55 11) 283-0515. Website: www.lhotel.com.br.* This is a real treat for travelers who are used to staying at the typical business or tourist hotel. Located in the heart of São Paulo, just off Avenida Paulista, L'Hotel is convenient to the business and shopping areas. An exclusive boutique hotel, the reception area has a European feel. Light colored marble clad walls and floor give an airy feel while the large oriental carpet on the floor and 16th century tapestry from Brussels mounted on the stairwell wall add warmth to the luxurious surroundings. The front desk staff welcomes guests with genuine warmth and go out of their way to be helpful and informative. If the people as well as the facilities make a fine hotel, L'Hotel is a winner in both categories. Each of the 78 guestrooms and 5 suites are elegantly decorated with floral print bedspreads, draperies, and matching cornice. The well-appointed compact marble bath offers expected amenities. The *Trebbiano* restaurant offers classic, authentic Italian cuisine; The *Piano Bar* offers the aura of a British club. Health/Fitness Center; Business Center; Meeting Facilities.

❑ **Sheraton Mofarrej Hotel:** *Alameda Santos, 1437, Cerqueira César, São Paulo, Brazil, Tel. (55 11) 253-5544, Fax (55 11) 289-8670, or toll-free from U.S. or Canada 800-325-3589. Website: www.sheraton.com.* Located in the heart of the city's business and financial district, near museums, theaters, commercial centers and restaurants, the Sheraton Mofarrej offers 244 nicely decorated and equipped guestrooms and suites. The 35 luxury suites, as well as guestrooms on the executive floors, come equipped with an office jet fax, printer, and scanner – ready for connection to a laptop, as well as butler service. Non-smoking rooms are available as well as rooms for physically disabled guests. *Restaurante Christine's* serves international cuisine and on Saturdays a typical Brazilian meal – *feijoada* – is served from noon to 3:00pm. The *Vivaldi Room* on the 23rd floor serves Sunday brunch along with a spectacular view. Fitness Center; Business Center; Convention and Banquet Facilities.

❑ **Renaissance São Paulo:** *Alameda Santos, 2233, São Paulo, SP, Brazil 01419-002, Tel. (55 11) 3069-2233, Fax (55 11) 3064-3344, or toll-free from U.S. or Canada 800-468-3571. Website: www.renaissancehotels.com.* Located in an area of tree-lined streets, elegant residences, exclusive boutiques along with some of the country's largest international trade, commercial and banking firms, the 27 floors of the Renaissance São Paulo offer 452 spacious guestrooms and 57 luxurious suites. Seven floors are for non-smoking guests. The six Renaissance Club floors offer private check-in/out; upgraded amenities; complimentary continental breakfast and evening hors d'oeuvres. Two restaurants serve a variety of cuisines in an indoor or al fresco setting. Fitness Facilities; Business Center; Conference and Banquet Facilities.

❑ **Transamérica:** *Av. das Nações Unidas 18591, Santo Amaro, São Paulo, Brazil 04795-901, Tel. (55 11) 5693-4511, Fax (55 11) 5693-4990. Website: www.transamerica.com.br.* Proud of its ISO 9002 certification and a member of "The Leading Hotels of the World," the Transamérica is located outside Centro near several business concentration areas. Surrounded by an extensive green area, the setting evokes tranquility in the city. The lobby is large and clad in beige marble. The hotel features 400 spacious guestrooms and suites with all expected conveniences including in-room workstations. Marble bathrooms include expected amenities. Two floors are available for non-smokers. The Golden Class floor provides private check-in/out, a private room for meetings, dining room, exclusive breakfast area, exclusive lounge, happy hour and butler service. *Anturius Restaurant* and *Blooming* offer a range of dining options including the traditional Brazilian *feijoada* and brunch. Health/Fitness Facilities; Business Center; Conference and Banquet Facilities.

❑ **Maksoud Plaza:** *Alameda Campinas, 150, São Paulo, SP, Brazil 01404-900, Tel. (55 11) 253-4411, Fax (55 11) 253-4544, or toll free from U.S. or Canada 800-223-6800. Website: www.maksoud.com.br.* Located in the heart of São Paulo, just off Avenida Paulista, the Maksoud Plaza is a member of "The Leading Hotels of the World." Upon entering the lobby, the guest is greeted by a soaring atrium lobby with panoramic elevators, greenery, fountains and shops. The 420 guestrooms and suites all feature a king size or two queen size beds. In-room computer services are available on request. There are two Presidential floors with butler service. Six restaurants offer diners a choice of cuisines. *La Cuisine du Soleil* serves a variety of cuisines. *Brasserie Belavista* serves a complete menu around the clock. The *Seafood Mezzanino* serves grilled seafood and Japanese specialties. *Arlanza Grill* presents selected grilled meats, fish and poultry. *Vikings* offers a Scandinavian smorgasbord, while *Pizzeria Belavista* serves crispy pizzas around the clock. The *Patisserie* has bakery delicacies available 24 hours a day. Health/Fitness Center; Business Center; Performing Arts Theater; Conference and Banquet Facilities. Popular with tour groups and airline personnel. Includes an excellent art, sculpture, and handicraft shop to the right of the entrance, **Reflexus**.

❑ **Inter-Continental São Paulo:** *Av. Santos 1123, São Paulo, Brazil 01419-001, Tel. (55 11) 3179-2600, Fax (55 11) 3179-2666. Website: www.interconti.com.* This attractive hotel offers 193 guestrooms and 37 suites. Both the public spaces and guestrooms are well appointed and all rooms have facilities for work stations. Club floors offer additional amenities. *Tarsila Restaurant.* Health/Fitness Facilities; Business Services; Conference and Banquet Facilities.

You'll find several other hotels throughout the city. For a quick reference, visit this website:

www.brazil.org.uk

Most major hotels in São Paulo also have their own websites. In addition to the above hotels, check out these hotel websites:

Augusta Boulevard:	*www.redepandehoteis.com.br*
Best Western Porto do Sol São Paulo:	*www.portodosol.com.br*
Blue Tree Caesar Towers Berrini:	*www.bluetree.com.br*
Blue Tree Caesar Towers Vila Olimpia:	*www.caesartowers.com.br*
Bourbon:	*www.bourbon.com.br*
Brasilton São Paulo:	*www.hilton.com*
Caesar Park:	*www.caesarpark.com.br*
Century Paulista:	*www.centuryflat.com.br*
Columbia:	*www.hotelcolumbia.com.br*
Comfort Hotel e Suites Trianon Park:	*www.choiceatlantica.com*
Crown Plaza:	*www.crowneplaza.com.br*
Eldorado Boulevard:	*www.hoteiseldorado.com.br*
Eldorado Higienópolis:	*www.hoteiseldorado.com.br*
Excelsior:	*www.hotelexcelsiorsp.com.br*
Free:	*www.freesp.com*
Grand Hotel Ca'd'Oro:	*www.cadoro.com.br*
Grand Hotel Mercure:	*www.accorbrasil.com.br*
Ibis São Paulo Expo:	*www.ibis-brasil.com.br*
Jandaia:	*www.hoteljandaia.com.br*
Linson:	*www.llinson.com.br*
Marian Palace:	*www.mandic.com.br/marian*
Nacional Inn:	*www.nacional-inn.com.br*
Novotel São Paulo Morumbi:	*www.accorbrasil.com.br*
Osaka Plaza:	*www.hotelosaka.com.br*
Othon Palace São Paulo:	*www.hoteis-othon.com.br*
Pan Americano:	*www.redepandehoteis.com.br*
Pão de Açúcar:	*www.hotelpaoacucar.com.br*
Park Lane:	*www.parklane.com.br*
Park Way All Suite:	*www.parkwayallsuite.com.br*
Paulista Plaza:	*www.goldentulip.com*
Plaza Apolo:	*www.harsa.com*
Plaza Arouche:	*www.plazaarouche.com.br*
Plaza Marabá:	*www.plazamaraba.com.br*
Real Castilha:	*www.realcastilha.com.br*
Regent Park:	*www.regent.com.br*
Requint:	*www.requint.com.br*
Rojas:	*www.rojas.com.br*
San Juan:	*www.sanjuanhoteis.com*
São Paulo Hilton:	*www.hilton.com*
San Raphael:	*www.sanraphael.com.br*
Sofitel São Paulo:	*www.accorbrasil.com.br*
Tropical Planalto:	*www.tropicalhotel.com.br*

West Side Suite: ***www.westsidesuitehotel. com.br***

RESTAURANTS

São Paulo is all about shopping *and* dining. And when it comes to dining, São Paulo easily gets the vote for being the gastronomic capital of Brazil. With more than 12,000 restaurants and 36 different cuisines, your dining choices here are simply overwhelming. In fact, in 1997 the Congress of International Hospitality, Food and Tourism named São Paulo as the "World Capital of Gastronomy." Not surprisingly, given São Paulo's large number of Italian, Japanese, and Middle Eastern immigrants, you'll find numerous Italian, Japanese, Arab, and Lebanese restaurants in the city. But the city also boasts many excellent French, Portuguese, and Brazilian restaurants as well as pizzerias and *churrascarias*. Dining in São Paulo tends to be informal and the dress code is at best smart casual. If you are a lifestyle shopper, who enjoys combining shopping with dining, you're in for a real treat in São Paulo. It simply doesn't get much better than in São Paulo.

❏ São Paulo is the gastronomic capital of Brazil with more than 12,000 restaurants and 36 different cuisines.

❏ Dining in São Paulo tends to be informal and at best smart casual.

❏ Some restaurants do not accept credit cards and some are closed on Sunday.

Since some restaurants do not accept credit cards and others add a credit card surcharge, check on payment methods when you make reservations or before being seated. Some restaurants are closed on Sundays, so be sure to call and make reservations for Sunday dining. As in other cities, Wednesdays and Saturdays are popular *feijoada* days in São Paulo.

BRAZILIAN

❏ **Baby Beef Rubaiyat:** *Alameda Santos, 86 (Cerqueira César), Tel. 289-6366.* This popular Brazilian restaurant serves numerous grilled items and a tempting salad bar. Friday is seafood day and Wednesdays and Saturdays are for *feijoadas*.

❏ **Esplanada Grill:** *Rua Haddock Lobo 1682 (Cerqueira César), Tel. 881-3199.* This popular churrascaria attracts many well-heeled locals. Try the *picanha* steak and *pão queijo* (cheese bread).

❏ **Bargaço:** *Rua Oscar Freire, 1189 (Cerqueira César), Tel. 853-5058.* Serves excellent Bahian and spicy seafood dishes. Try the shrimp and fish *moquecas* as well as *carne-de-sol* with mashed manioc and milk and the grilled sampler.

❏ **Dona Lucinha:** *Av. Chibarás, 399 (Moema), Tel. 549-2050; and Rua Bela Cintra, 2325 (Cerqueria César), Tel. 282-3797.* Serves excellent buffet-style *bineiro* cuisine from the Minas Gerais State. Includes more than 50 dishes.

❏ **Consulado Mineiro:** *Rua Praça Benedito Calixto, 74 (Pinheiros), Tel. 3064-3882.* This traditional Minas Gerais restaurant serves excellent bean *tropeiro* and pork *à pururuca*. Especially popular on Saturday afternoon.

CONTINENTAL

❏ **Cantaloup:** *Rua Manoel Guedes, 474 (Itaim Bibi), Tel. 866-6445.* Arguably São Paulo's best restaurant with lots of great ambience for an evening of romantic dining in a converted old warehouse. Everything here is excellent, from meat to fish to pasta dishes. Includes lots of interesting fusion cuisine. Excellent presentation of dishes.

ITALIAN

❏ **Fasano:** *Rua Haddock Lobo, 1644 (Jardins), Tel. 852-4000.* This also is arguably the best restaurant in São Paulo. Popular with the rich, famous, and "beautiful people" who park their Porsches and Ferraris out front, this long established Northern Italian eatery also boasts some of the most expensive dining in São Paulo – expect to pay US$60 to US$80 per person without wine, including one of the highest "couvert" charges in Brazil (R$13 per person). It also offers a set price three-course dinner for under R$100 per person. Since menus are in Portuguese and Italian, you may want the head waiter to translate the dishes on the menu if these are not your languages. Nice ambience, especially in the rear dining room. Boasts one of the best wine cellars in the city.

❏ **Lellis Trattoria:** *Rua Bela Cintra, 1849 (Jardim Paulista), Tel. 3064-2727.* Are you hungry for Italian cuisine? Here's the ultimate solution! This well established traditional Italian cantina serves really huge portions (tip – plan to split your entree). Interesting, borderline tacky, setting which includes photos of famous locals and walls and ceilings of wine bottles.

Expect a very crowded and noisy atmosphere – the focus here is on the mountains of food. The salmon filet *mirinata* is especially good. Good value but watch your check and wine – you might experience "slippage" with the wrong prices listed (not to your advantage) and substituted wine (not the quality you ordered). But the food is good and the wine is not bad, if they get it right!

❑ **Massimo:** *Alameda Santos, 1826 (Jardins), Tel. 284-0311.* Popular with the business crowd around Avenida Paulista and VIPs. Try the leg of lamb or cod filet with tomato and black olives.

❑ **Famiglia Mancini:** *Rua Avanhandava, 81 (Centro), Tel. 256-4320.* Serves excellent pasta and a wonderful buffet spread of appetizers. Especially crowded late at night.

❑ **Ca'D'Oro:** *Grande Hotel Ca' D'Oro, Rua Augusta, 129 (Bela Vista), Tel. 236-4300.* This popular Northern Italian restaurant specializes in *bollieto mist* and *casonci à la bergamassa*.

❑ **La Vecchia Cucina:** *Rua Pedroso Alvarenga, 1088 (Itaim), Tel. 3060-9822.* This well appointed restaurant especially appeals to a well-heeled client. Try the duck ravioli with watercress sauce, frog risotto, or sliced duck with citric fruit and rose peppers and smoked eel.

FRENCH

❑ **Le Coq Hardy:** *Rua Jerônimo da Veiga, 461 (Itaim), Tel. 852-3344.* This popular restaurant is noted for its fine chefs who produce excellent escalope de foie gras, cassoulet de scargot, tartufo, and pheasant aux Murielle. Be sure to try the hot chocolate cake dessert. Offers classic French cuisine. Very expensive.

❑ **Laurent:** *Alameda Jaú, 1606, Flat Residência Paulista (Cerqueira César), Tel. 853-5574.* Especially popular for lunch with businesspeople – try the executive menu which is good value. Chef's specialties include *canard* or *tucupi* and *baclhau* (codfish) in spinach leaves.

❑ **La Casserole:** *Largo do Arouche, 346 (Centro), Tel. 220-6283.* This long-established French bistro is noted for its classic French dishes and cozy setting.

❏ **Freddy:** *Praça Dom Gastão Liberal Pinto, 111 (Itaim), Tel. 829-0977.* Another long-established French bistro serving excellent classic French dishes. Try the pheasant with herb sauce or cassoulet.

❏ **Charlô:** *Rua Barão de Capanema, 440 (Jardins), Tel. 280-6790.* This cozy French bistro makes an ideal stop for lunch while shopping in the Cerqueira César/Jardins area. Offers a good selection of sandwiches. Can dine inside or outside along the sidewalk.

JAPANESE

❏ **Saushi-Yassu:** *Rua Tomás Gonzaga, 110A (Liberdade), Tel. 279-6030.* Serves excellent sushi. Try the ginger shrimp with Pacific salmon.

❏ **Sushi Yassu:** *Rua Tomás Gonzaga, 98 (Liberdade), Tel. 279-6030.* Serves excellent sushi and fish dishes. Try the ginger shrimp with Pacific salmon.

❏ **Roppongi:** *Rua Jorge Coelho, 128 (Itaim), Tel. 883-6991.* Attracts an upmarket crowd who enjoy the nice mixture of eastern and western flavors. Popular sushi bar.

PORTUGUESE

❏ **Antiquarius:** Alameda Lorena, 1884 (Cerqueira César), Tel. 282-3015. Sister restaurant to the famous Portuguese restaurant with the same name in Rio. Serves excellent dishes in a formal setting. Try the fresh cod *moqueca*, rice with shredded duck, or leg of lamb.

❏ **Presidente:** *Rua Visconde de Parnaiba, 2424 (Belenzinho), Tel. 292-8683.* This long-established restaurant continues to service excellent Portuguese dishes. Cod, in several varieties, is one of the house specialties.

SPANISH

❏ **Dalí:** *Rua Martinho Augusto Rodriques, 49 (Itaim), Tel. 852-5271.* The city's only Catalonian restaurant serves excellent seafood dishes such as lobster with chocolate sauce, baked cod, and *aglio olio* grilled seafood.

❑ **Don Curro:** *Rua Alves Guimarães, 230 (Jardim América), Tel. 852-4712.* Serves excellent paella.

❑ **La Coruña:** *Rua Prof. Arthur Ramos, 183 (Jardim Europa), Tel. 813-1232.* Known for its excellent Valencian paella. Also, try the shrimp á la Coruña.

Indian

❑ **Ganash:** *Av. Roque Petroni Jr., 1089, Shopping Morumbi, lj. 20/27 (Morumbi), Tel. 240-6768.* Serves excellent curry and tandoori dishes adjusted to Western tastes.

❑ **Govinda:** *Rua Princesa Isabel, 379 (Brooklin), Tel. 531-8587.* Reputed to be the first Indian restaurant in Latin America. Serves tandoori dishes.

Lebanese

❑ **Almanara:** *Rua Oscar Freire, 523 (Jardins), Tel. 853-6916.* A good place for lunch – try the hummus and grilled chicken. Serves excellent Lebanese specialties *rodizio*-style. Part of a Lebanese restaurant chain.

❑ **Arábia:** *Rua Haddock Lobo, 1397 (Cerqueira César), Tel. 3064-4776.* Serves excellent Lebanese and other Arab dishes in a pleasant setting. Try the *falafel* and *fatayer*.

Seafood

❑ **La Trainera:** *Av. Brigadeiro Faria Lima, 511 (Jardim Paulistano), Tel. 282-5988.* Serves excellent seafood dishes in three dining rooms. Includes many tempting variations of cod, shrimp, and lobster.

❑ **Amadeus:** *Rua Haddock Lobo, 807 (Jardins), Tel. 3061-2859.* Serves excellent dishes, from appetizers (salmon and oysters) to entrees (shrimp). Includes an open-air oyster bar and pianist in the evening.

Pizza

❑ **Babbo Giovanni:** *Rua Bela Cintra, 2305 (Cerqueira César), Tel. 853-3678.* This famous pizzeria turns out some of the city's best pizzas. Try the loaded Mamma Celeste.

❑ **Castelóes:** *Rus Jairo Góes, 126 (Brás), Tel. 229-0542.* The city's oldest pizzeria. Try the famous mozzarella pizzas.

❑ **Galpão:** *Rua Doutor Augusto de Miranda, 1156 (Pompéia), Tel. 262-4767.* Interesting architectural design adds atmosphere to this pizzeria. Try the mozzarella pizza.

SEEING THE SITES

While shopping and dining appear to be the favorite pastimes in São Paulo, there are also lots of sites to see for anyone interested in museums, churches, buildings, and parks. The city's major sightseeing highlights include the following:

MUSEUMS

❑ **MASP (São Paulo Art Museum):** *1578 Avenida Paulista, Tel. 251-5644. Open Monday through Friday, 11am - 3pm; Saturday and Sunday from 12noon - 4pm.* Located in the middle of Avenida Paulista, this is one of Brazil's top fine arts museums. Also known as the "Paulista" or "Ipiranga" museum, it houses a valuable collection of paintings, including such renowned artists as Picasso, Goya, Renoir, Velasquez, and Van Gogh. Musical performances often take place in the open space below the MASP museum. On Sunday a large antique fair (Antiquidades do MASP) is held at the open area at street level.

❑ **Museum of Contemporary Art (MAC):** *Rua da Reitoria, 160, Cidade Universitária, Tel. 818-3039. Open Monday to Friday, 12noon - 8pm; and Saturday, 9am - 1pm. Also includes two other locations – Rua da Reitoria, 109A (Anexo) and Pq. do Ibirapuera, Pavilhão da Bienal, 3rd floor.* Represents Latin America's largest collection of modern art with over 5,000 works of art. Includes works by Picasso, Kandinsky, Matisse, Modigliani, and Di Cavalcanti. Also includes an extensive library and data bank.

❑ **Museum of Modern Art (MAM):** *Pq. do Ibirapuera, Grande Marquise, Tel. 549-9688. Open Tuesday and Wednesday, 12noon - 6pm; Thursday, 12noon - 10pm; and Saturday and Sunday, 10am - 6pm.* The city's oldest museum of modern art with more than 2,500 works of art in the permanent collection, including an outdoor sculpture garden. Includes regular exhibitions.

❏ **Pinacoteca do Estado:** *Praça da Luz, 2 (Centro), Tel. 227-6329. Open Tuesday to Sunday, 10am - 6pm. Free admission on Thursday.* Located opposite Luz train station, this state gallery of art presents an excellent collection of Brazilian art. Includes a restaurant and gift shop.

❏ **Historical Museum of the Japanese Immigration to Brazil:** *Rua São Joaquim, 381, 7th and 8th floors (Liberdade), Tel. 279-5465. Open Tuesday to Sunday, 1:30pm - 5:30pm.* Documents the history of the Japanese in Brazil. Includes displays of antiques and Japanese contributions to Brazilian agriculture and horticulture.

❏ **Museum of the Memory of Bixiga:** *Rua dos Inglese, 118 (Bixiga), Tel. 285-5009. Open Wednesday to Sunday, 2pm - 5pm.* Presents a humorous tale of the local Italian community. A good time to visit is on Saturday or Sunday when the nearby arts and antiques market (Feira do Bixiga) operates at Praça Dom Orione.

❏ **House of Roses Museum:** *Avenida Paulista, 37 (Tel. 251-5271. Open Tuesday to Sunday, 12noon - 8pm.* The only remaining mansion along the street that once was the center for the mansions of the city's coffee barons. This restored three-story French Renaissance house showcases the architecture and life of a bygone era.

❏ **Sacred Art Museum:** *Avenida Tiradentes, 676 (Centro), Tel. 227-7694. Open Tuesday to Friday, 11am - 6pm, and Saturday and Sunday, 10am - 7pm.* Located within the Monastery of Luz, this is the museum of the convent that was originally constructed in 1774 and which still functions with 14 active nuns. Includes exhibits of religious art produced in Brazil beginning in the 16th century. Includes terracotta and wood carvings of Benedictine images.

BUILDINGS

São Paulo is a city of great buildings and architecture. Indeed, one of its major defining characteristics is its skyline of tall buildings. Visitors to this city especially find these buildings interesting enough to include them in their exploration of the city. Several buildings offer opportunities to get a panoramic view of the city from their top floors.

❑ **Italian Building (Edificio Itália):** *Avenida Ipiranga, 336 (Centro).* Great view of the city from the 41st floor Terraço Itália restaurant and bar. However, you'll need to patronize this rather mediocre but expensive restaurant to get the free view (Tel. 257-6566).

❑ **BANESPA Building (Edificio BANASPA):** *Praça Antônio Prado (Centro).* Constructed in 1947 in the image of New York City's Empire State Building, this building offers an excellent view of the city from its 36th floor.

❑ **Martinelli Building (Edificio Martinelli):** *Avenida São João, 35 (Centro).* This is the city's first skyscraper which was built in 1929 by Italian immigrant Giuseppe Martinelli. Good view of the city from the 36th floor observation deck (open 10:30am - 4pm).

❑ **Municipal Theatre (Teatro Municipal):** *Praça Ramos de Azevedo Square (Centro), Tel. 223-3022.* Copied after a Parisian theater and incorporating Baroque style and Art Nouveau elements, this is one of São Paulo's most famous buildings. It functions as a popular venue for dance performances and music concerts.

❑ **Industrial Palace:** *77 Rua da Figueira, Dom Pedro II Park (Centro), Tel. 3315-9077.* Extremely eclectic architecture defines this building which is now the mayor's office. Built in 1924 as an agro-industrial exposition center, the highlight of this building is the huge "Coffee Plantation" painting by Di Cavalcanti.

CHURCHES

Most of São Paulo's interesting churches are found in the Centro area. If you enjoy visiting old and architecturally interesting churches, as well as attend Sunday services in new places, you'll find several interesting churches here.

❑ **Metropolitan Cathedral of Sé (Catedral de Sé):** *Praça de Sé (Centro). Open 7:30am - 7pm, Tel. 3107-6832.* Located next to the Justice Place, this is the city's major church. Construction began in 1913 and was finally completed 40 years later. Boasts the largest Italian pipe organ (10,200 pipes) in Latin America.

❏ **Pátio do Colégio (College Courtyard):** *Pátio do Colégio, 84 (Centro), Tel. 3105-6899.* Jesuit missionaries built the first chapel of São Paulo here. The church, built in the same style as the chapel, was constructed in 1896.

❏ **São Bento Basílica and Monastery (Basilica de São Bento):** *Open daily, 6am - 12noon and 2pm - 6pm; closed for cleaning on Tuesday from 8am - 2pm.* Built between 1910 and 1922, this church is known for its baroque crucifix from 1777, Portuguese image of Our Lady of "Conceição," stained glass windows, carved choir stalls, and a fabulous German organ with 6,000 pipes.

Parks and Squares

❏ **Praça da República:** *Av. Ipiranga (Centro).* Once the residential center for the city's coffee barons with their huge mansions, this crowded area is now dominated by office buildings, hotels, shops, cinemas, and restaurants. A key landmark within the Centro district, this large square is the center for a lively Sunday arts and crafts market. Some vendors, including street artists, remain active all week long.

❏ **Praça da Sé:** *Located south of Pátio do Colégio (Centro).* This huge square, dominated by the neo-Gothic Catedral Metropolitana, is the center of colonial São Paulo. A lively area, the square is usually crowded with pedestrians, hawkers, street musicians, beggars, and homeless children. Just north of this square is the Municipal Market (Mercado Municipal), Municipal Theater (Teatro Municipal), and one of the city's newest and most upscale shopping centers, Shopping Light.

❏ **Praça da Luz:** *Located north of Avenida Tiradentes. Open 10am - 6pm.* Once the city's grand and green park, with attractive gardens, ponds, bandstand, and wrought-iron fence, it is increasingly becoming a popular leisure area for local residents. Includes many outdoor sculptures.

❏ **Parque Siqueira Campos:** *Avenida Paulista and across the street from MASP. Open 6am - 9pm.* This small but inviting park is a delightful place to explore for its trees, foliage and trails. On Sundays the entrance to this park becomes the center for a lively arts and crafts market that also includes food vendors and talented street musicians who perform as well as offer their CDs at bargain prices.

❑ **Ibirapuera Park:** *Avenida Pedro Álvares Cabral (Ibirapuera), Tel. 575-5511. Open 6am - 10pm* Located southeast of the Jardins, this is the city's largest (1.6 million square meters) and most popular park which was designed by architect Oscar Niemeyer and landscape artist Roberto Burle Marx to celebrate the city's 400th anniversary in 1954. It encompasses the Legislative Assembly, planetarium, and several museums (Museu de Arte Contemporânea, Museu de Arte Moderna, and Museu de Folclore) as well as the city's indoor sports center, a velodrome for cycle racing, sports fields, jogging paths, playgrounds, hothouse, and Sunday concerts in Praça da Paz. The huge shopping center, Shopping Ibirapuera, is located nearby.

❑ **Praça Liberdade:** *Located at the intersection of Avenida de Liberdade and Rua Galvao Bueno (Liberdade).* On Sundays this square becomes the center for a lively arts, crafts, and food market.

❑ **Independence Park (Parque da Independência):** *Located in the suburb of Ipiranga, 5 kilometers southeast of Centro.* Includes the Independence Monument (Monumento à Independência), tomb of Brazil's first emperor (Dom Pedro I) and empress (Leopoldina).

❑ **Botanic Garden (Jardim Botânico):** *Avenida Miguel Stefano (Água Funda). Open Wednesday to Sunday, 9am - 5pm.* Includes a botanic museum, the Botanic Institute, lakes, and gardens spread over a 360,000 square meter area.

❑ **Zoo:** *Avenida Miguel Stefano, 4241 (Água Funda), Tel. 276-0811. Open Tuesday to Sunday, 9am - 5pm.* Includes over 5,000 animals, from birds to reptiles. Most can be observed in their natural habitat. Ranked by some experts as one of the world's five best zoos.

ENTERTAINMENT

In addition to spending evenings dining in some of São Paulo's top restaurants, you'll find lots of bars, nightclubs, cinemas, and theaters to occupy your evenings after what hopefully has been a productive day of lifestyle shopping and sightseeing. Many of the bars include restaurants, live music, dance floors, fireplaces, outdoor tables, and lots of beer. Here are some of the city's most popular evening entertainment spots:

BARS

❑ **Brahma:** *Avenida São João, 677 (Centro), Tel. 223-6720. Open Saturday and Monday to Thursday, 11am - midnight; and Friday, 11am - 1am.* One of the city's most traditional bars serving excellent beers. Includes a restaurant, piano bar, America bar, and sidewalk tables.

❑ **Balcão:** *Rua Doutor Melo Alves, 150 (Cerqueira César), Tel. 380-4630.* A trendy bar with a well-heeled clientele in one of the city's most attractive neighborhoods.

❑ **Barnaldo Lucrecia:** *Rua Abílio Soares, 207 (Paraiso), Tel. 885-3425.* Draws a young and lively crowd that enjoys live MPB. Especially popular on Friday evenings.

❑ **Charles Edward & CIA:** *Avenida Pres. Juscelino Kubitschek, 1426 (Itaim), Tel. 820-9803. Open Monday to Friday, 6pm to 2:30am, and Saturday, 5pm - 2:30am.* A former antique shop converted to a bar, this place appeals to the 30s and 40s crowd. Includes live music and dancing.

❑ **Finnegan's:** *Alameda Itu, 1529 (Cerqueira César), Tel. 853-7852; and Rua Cristiano Viana, 358 (Pinheiros), Tel. 852-3232. Open Monday to Wednesday, 6pm - 2am; Thursday and Friday, 6pm - 3am; and Sunday, 5pm - 2am.* Includes two sections – an Irish-style pub and a French/Swiss restaurant. Often includes blues and jazz music.

❑ **Original:** *Rua Graúna, 137 (Moema), Tel. 530-9486.* One of the city's original "traditional bars" with an attractive 1940s atmosphere. Serves excellent draft beer.

❑ **Pirajá:** *Avenida Brigadeiro Faria Lima 64 (Pinheiros), Tel. 815-6881.* This trendy "traditional bar" packs in crowds in the early evening. Known for serving excellent Spanish tapas.

NIGHTCLUBS

❑ **Clube B.A.S.E.:** *Avenida Brigadeiro Luis Antônio, 1137 (Bela Vista), Tel. 605-3162. Open Monday to Saturday, 9pm until everyone leaves.* This popular nightclub includes three bars and a huge dance floor capable of accommodating 1,300 people.

❑ **Brancaleone:** *Rua Luis Murat, 298 (Jardim América), Tel. 870-8873. Open Monday to Saturday, 5:30pm - 3am.* Music venues change nightly – disco, soul, Brazilian pop, forró, rock, 70's funk, and acid jazz.

❑ **Columbia:** *Rua Estados Unidos, 1570 (Cerqueira César), Tel. 282-8086.* Offers four different entertainment venues which include a brewery, bars, and discos.

❑ **Lov.e Club & Lounge:** *Rua Pequetita, 189 (Vila Olímpia), Tel. 3044-1613. Open Tuesday to Friday, midnight - 6am, and Saturday, midnight - 10am.* Plan to stay until early morning and have breakfast at this funky techno nightclub.

BEYOND SÃO PAULO

Plan to spend at least a day exploring areas outside São Paulo. While this city does not have the beaches and mountains of Rio, the beaches (port of Santos and the North Shore) and mountains (Serra da Cantareira) are not far from the city. Indeed, within a one-hour drive you can find beaches that are equal to those found in and around Rio (try the popular North Shore beaches of Camburi, Maresias, and Ubatuba).

If you enjoy shopping, and especially visiting interesting colonial towns with antique shops and arts and crafts markets, plan side trips to two nearby towns which are very popular with weekend shoppers – Itu and Embu. Located within 45 minutes of São Paulo, these two towns are delightful places to explore.

The best way to get to these places is to rent a car from one of the many rental firms (Avis, Hertz, Budget, Localiza) found along the 300 and 400 blocks of Rua da Consolação in Centro. Budget Rent-a-Car, for example, charges around R$80 a day for a small car. From Centro, it's relatively easy to get in and out of the city by car on a weekend. Pick it up on Saturday morning and return it late Sunday afternoon or arrange to have it picked up at your hotel on Sunday evening or Monday morning. However, avoid driving in the crowded city during weekdays.

ITU

Located 90 kilometers northwest of São Paulo, this charming old Portuguese colonial town once played important roles in the Brazilian republican movement. Founded in 1610 and variously becoming a city for textile and coffee production during the 18th and 19th centuries, today Itu is a large town noted for its old churches, antique shops, tourists, and tendency to exaggerate everything, especially in products that symbolize the city, including the size of traffic lights and pay phones. The reputation for exaggeration is especially noted in souvenir shops that offer oversized pencils, huge hats and combs, large sheets of money, and gigantic cigarettes and condoms – anything that symbolizes the town's tendency to exaggerate everything. This exaggeration theme relates to the antics of a local comedian in the 1960s whose routine stressed how much bigger and better Itu was compared to other places in Brazil.

You can easily spend two to three hours in this town just exploring its many crowded antique shops which are primarily found adjacent to each other along one street – **Rua Paula Souza**. In fact, you may want to pick up a tourist map of the town which is available in several shops (look for them near the entrance of the shops). The following shops are worth visiting:

❑ **Antiquário Tempo do Onça:** *Rua Paula Souza, 687, Tel. 7822-8500.* Includes several rooms of antique furniture, clocks, porcelain, pots, and collectibles.

❑ **Itu-Antigo:** *Rua Paula Souza, 655, Tel. 7822-1212.* One of the best antique shops in Itu with three levels of furniture, pots, pictures, and ceramics. Attractive setting with an outdoor courtyard.

❑ **Antiquário Lila:** *Rua Paula Souza, 607, Tel. 7822-0288.* This huge shop, which is a charming old house, seems to go on and on with its two levels with numerous rooms filled with antique furniture, bowls, glass, tiles, hats, helmets, chandeliers, telephones, radios, paintings, glassware, copper pots, garden pieces, instruments, religious figures, and other collectibles.

❑ **Antiquidades e Construções Coloniais:** *Rua Dom Manoel da Silveira D'Elboux, 214, Tel. 7822-1061.* This tiny corner shop (faces Rua Paula Souza) includes many surprises, from pots and paintings to furniture and toys. Includes many nice pots, but you'll need to dig around all the furniture to find the full inventory of pots.

❑ **A. R. Antiguidades:** *Rua Paula Souza, 558, Tel. 7823-0347.* Includes lots of antique furniture, china, glassware, pots, and collectibles.

❑ **Vitri 'Italia:** *Rua Paula Souza, 546, Tel. 7822-2609.* This is an unusual shop in the midst of traditional antique shops. The main product lines here are Italian-style art deco, nuevo art tables, chairs, clocks, lamps, lanterns, stained glass. Includes lots of iron furniture for gardens or gazebos as well as beautiful stained glass screens and window panels.

❑ **Casa Amarela:** *Rua Dos Andradas, 306, Tel. 7822-4918.* Located on the next street parallel to Rua Paula Souza, this antique shop includes several rooms of quality furniture, silver, and glassware.

Also, be sure to explore the nearby town square (Praça Pde. Miguel) which includes several outdoor cafes, shops, and street vendors. The **Grande Shop** includes many souvenirs commemorating the city's reputation for exaggeration.

EMBU

Located 27 kilometers west of São Paulo, this large Portuguese colonial town of 200,000 residents is famous for its artists and craftspeople who also operate furniture, antique, art, and handicrafts stores and stalls. They also operate a very popular and expansive Sunday arts and crafts market that attracts numerous visitors. The Sunday market here is very large compared to many you may have visited elsewhere in Brazil. If, for example, you went to the popular Hippie Fair in Rio, you'll find Embu's Sunday market at least 10 times as large.

If you're primarily interested in antiques, be sure to visit Embu on Saturday since many antique shops close on Sunday when the town takes on a decidedly festive arts, crafts, food, and trash-and-treasures atmosphere. Indeed, on Sunday, from 9am to 6pm, the town transforms itself into a huge pedestrian mall as thousands of people descend on the town to shop its many vendor street stalls and permanent shops along its traffic-free streets. It's a good idea to arrive in Embu early on Sunday – by 9:30am – to get a convenient parking place near the market area since the market becomes very busy around 11am. As you drive to the central parking area, you'll pass several furniture shops which offer a variety of rustic country furniture which may or may not appeal to your decorating tastes. The more interesting permanent art galleries and antique, arts, crafts, jewelry, and souvenir shops are found in and around the pedestrian market area. You're bound to find something of interest here, from paintings, clothes, ceramics, and jams to candles, belts, T-shirts, and plants. But don't come here with great shopping expectations. While many of the art galleries, handicrafts shops, and arts and crafts stalls offer good quality, unique items, you'll also find lots of tourist kitsch here, including a great deal of forgettable flea market junk. For many visitors, the food stalls are the highlight of this town. The market area seems to go on forever, up cobblestone streets and through narrow walkways. This is a good place to just enjoy a leisurely Sunday exploring shops, stalls, and restaurants in a pleasant colonial setting. Some of our favorite permanent shops include:

❑ **Emporio São Pedro:** *Rua Siqueira Campos, Viela das Lavadeiras, 28, Tel. 7961-2797.* Located along a narrow side street off the main street, this small, intimate, and highly eclectic restaurant and art shop is a great place to dine, shop, and chat with the owner. Enjoy some wonderful pasta dishes as you listen to music by Frank Sinatra, Tony Bennett, and Billy Holiday and shop for wood carvings, glassware, and other arts and crafts. Includes both inside and outside dining areas. Will accommodate groups of up to 10 for dinner. Delightful owner shares his tips on the town.

❑ **Malyla's:** *Rua N. Sra. Do Rosário, 42, Tel. 494-3984.* Includes lots of nice antiques, furniture, pots, carpets, and collectibles.

❑ **Clarice Antiquidades:** *Rua N. Sra. Do Rosário, 116, Tel. 494-6071.* Offers a good selection of furniture, pots, wood bowls, and antique meat grinders.

❑ **São Martinho Antiguidades:** *Rua Joaquim Santana, 55, Tel. 494-4394.* Includes a good selection of furniture, pots, glassware, and even African masks.

❑ **Inca:** *Rua Padre Belchior de Pontes, 28, Tel. 494-3588.* This large shop includes a wide selection of handicrafts and souvenirs.

The problem of visiting Itu and Embu on the weekends is that visits to these two towns can compete directly with time for visiting the weekend markets in São Paulo. Since these towns are within a one-hour drive of Centro, you may want to visit Itu on Saturday afternoon and Embu on Sunday morning (arrive by 9:30am and leave by 12noon, arriving back in São Paulo by 12:30pm). That way you'll have at least a half day left for visiting São Paulo's popular markets. The biggest problem is on Sunday – working your schedule so that you·can do both Embu's and São Paulo's popular Sunday markets. Keep in mind that Embu's market closes at 6pm and São Paulo's markets close between 4pm and 6pm, depending on the particular market.

Index

SÃO PAULO

The Authors

W INSTON CHURCHILL PUT IT BEST – *"My needs are very simple – I simply want the best of everything."* Indeed, his attitude on life is well and alive amongst many of today's travelers. With limited time, careful budgeting, and a sense of adventure, many people seek both quality and value as they search for the best of the best.

Ron and Caryl Krannich, Ph.Ds, discovered this fact of travel life 18 years ago when they were living and working in Thailand as consultants with the Office of the Prime Minister. Former university professors and specialists on Southeast Asia, they discovered what they really loved to do – shop for quality arts, antiques, and home decorative items – was not well represented in most travel guides that primarily focused on sightseeing, hotels, and restaurants. While some guidebooks included a small section on shopping, they only listed types of products and names and addresses of a few shops, many of questionable quality. And budget guides simply avoided quality shopping altogether, as if shopping was a travel sin!

The Krannichs knew there was much more to travel than what was represented in most travel guides. Avid collectors of Asian, South Pacific, Middle Eastern, and Latin American arts, antiques, and home decorative items, they learned long ago that one of the best ways to experience another culture and meet its talented artists and craftspeople was by shopping for local products. Not only would they learn a great deal about the culture and society, they also acquired some wonderful products, met many interesting and talented individuals, and helped support the continuing development of local arts and crafts.

But they quickly learned shopping in many countries was very different from shopping in North America and Europe. In the West, merchants nicely display items, identify prices, and periodically run sales. At the same time, shoppers in the West can easily do comparative shopping, watch for sales, and trust quality and delivery; they even have consumer protection! Americans and Europeans in other parts of the world face a shopping culture based on different principles. Like a fish out of water, they make many mistakes: don't know how to bargain, avoid purchasing large items because they don't understand shipping, and are frequent victims of scams and rip-offs, especially in the case of gems and jewelry. To shop a country right, travelers need to know how to find quality products, bargain for the best prices, avoid scams, and ship their purchases with ease. What they most need is a combination travel and how-to book that focuses on the best of the best.

In 1987 the Krannichs inaugurated their first shopping guide to Asia – *Shopping in Exotic Places* – a guide to quality shopping in Hong Kong, South Korea, Thailand, Indonesia, and Singapore. Receiving rave reviews from leading travel publications and professionals, the book quickly found an enthusiastic audience amongst other avid travel-shoppers. It broke new ground as a combination travel and how-to book. No longer would shopping be confined to just naming products and identifying names and addresses of shops. It also included advice on how to pack for a shopping trip (take two suitcases, one filled with bubble-wrap), comparative shopping, bargaining skills, and shopping rules. Shopping was serious stuff requiring serious treatment of the subject by individuals who understood what they were doing. The Krannichs subsequently expanded the series to include separate volumes on Hong Kong, Thailand, Indonesia, Singapore and Malaysia, Australia and Papua New Guinea, the South Pacific, and the Caribbean.

Beginning in 1996, the series took on a new look as well as an expanded focus. Known as the Impact Guides and appropriately titled *The Treasures and Pleasures of . . . Best of the Best*, new editions covered Hong Kong, Thailand, Indonesia, Singapore, Malaysia, Paris and the French Riviera, and the Caribbean. In 1997 and 1999 new volumes appeared on Italy,

Hong Kong, and China. New volumes for 2000 and 2001 covered India, Australia, Thailand, Hong Kong, Singapore and Bali, Egypt, Israel and Jordan, Rio and São Paulo, Morocco, Vietnam, Indonesia, and the Philippines.

The Impact Guides now serve as the major content for the new travel-shopping website appropriately called *i*ShopAround TheWorld:

www.ishoparoundtheworld.com

While the primary focus remains shopping for quality products, the books and website also include useful information on the best hotels, restaurants, and sightseeing. As the authors note, *"Our users are discerning travelers who seek the best of the best. They are looking for a very special travel experience which is not well represented in other travel guides."*

The Krannichs passion for traveling and shopping is well represented in their home which is uniquely designed around their Asian, South Pacific, Middle East, North African, and Latin American art collections and which has been featured on CNN. *"We're fortunate in being able to create a living environment which pulls together so many wonderful travel memories and quality products,"* say the Krannichs. *"We learned long ago to seek out quality products and buy the best we could afford at the time. Quality lasts and is appreciated for years to come. Many of our readers share our passion for quality shopping abroad."* Their books also are popular with designers, antique dealers, and importers who use them to source products and suppliers.

While the Impact Guides keep the Krannichs busy traveling to exotic places, their travel series is an avocation rather than a vocation. The Krannichs also are noted authors of more than 30 career books, some of which deal with how to find international and travel jobs. The Krannichs also operate one of the world's largest career resource centers. Their works are available in most bookstores or through the publisher's online bookstore: *www.impactpublications.com*

If you have any questions or comments for the authors, please direct them to the publisher:

Ron and Caryl Krannich
IMPACT PUBLICATIONS
9104 Manassas Drive, Suite N
Manassas Park, VA 20111-5211 USA
Fax 703-335-9486
Email: *krannich@impactpublications.com*

Feedback and Recommendations

WE WELCOME FEEDBACK AND RECOMMEN-
dations from our readers and users. If you have
encountered a particular shop or travel experience, both good or bad, that you feel should be
included in future editions of this book or on
www.ishoparoundtheworld.com, please send your comments by
email, fax, or mail to:

Ron and Caryl Krannich
IMPACT PUBLICATIONS
9104 Manassas Drive, Suite N
Manassas Park, VA 20111-5211 USA
Fax 703-335-9486
Email: *krannich@impactpublications.com*

_____

_____

_____

_____

_____

_____

_____

_____

More Treasures
and Pleasures

THE FOLLOWING TRAVEL GUIDES CAN BE OR-
dered directly from the publisher. Complete the following form (or list the titles), include your name and
address, enclose payment, and send your order to:

IMPACT PUBLICATIONS
9104 Manassas Drive, Suite N
Manassas Park, VA 20111-5211 (USA)
Tel. 1-800-361-1055 (orders only)
703-361-7300 (information) Fax 703-335-9486
E-mail: *rio@impactpublications.com*
Online bookstores: ***www.impactpublications.com*** or
www.ishoparoundtheworld.com

All prices are in U.S. dollars. Orders from individuals should be
prepaid by check, moneyorder, or credit card (we accept Visa,
MasterCard, American Express, and Discover). We accept
credit card orders by telephone, fax, e-mail, and online (visit
Impact's two online travel bookstores). If your order must be
shipped outside the U.S., please include an additional US$1.50
per title for surface mail or the appropriate air mail rate for
books weighting 24 ounces each. Orders usually ship within 48
hours. For more information on the authors, travel resources,
and international shopping, visit ***www.impactpublications.com***
and ***www.ishoparoundtheworld.com*** on the World Wide Web.

Qty.	TITLES	Price	TOTAL
__	Air Traveler's Survival Guide	$14.95	_____
__	The Traveling Woman	$14.95	_____
__	Travel Planning on the Internet	$19.95	_____
__	Treasures and Pleasures of Australia	$17.95	_____
__	Treasures and Pleasures of the Caribbean	$16.95	_____
__	Treasures and Pleasures of China	$14.95	_____
__	Treasures and Pleasures of Egypt	$16.95	_____

__ Treasures and Pleasures of Hong Kong	$16.95	_____
__ Treasures and Pleasures of India	$16.95	_____
__ Treasures and Pleasures of Indonesia	$16.95	_____
__ Treasures and Pleasures of Israel & Jordan	$16.95	_____
__ Treasures and Pleasures of Italy	$14.95	_____
__ Treasures and Pleasures of Morocco	$16.95	_____
__ Treasures and Pleasures of Paris and the French Riviera	$14.95	_____
__ Treasures and Pleasures of the Philippines	$16.95	_____
__ Treasures and Pleasures of Rio/São Paulo	$13.95	_____
__ Treasures and Pleasures of Singapore/Bali	$16.95	_____
__ Treasures and Pleasures of Thailand	$16.95	_____
__ Treasures and Pleasures of Vietnam	$16.95	_____

SUBTOTAL ------------ $ _____

■ Virginia residents add 4.5% sales tax $ _____

■ Shipping/handling ($5.00 for the first
  title and $1.50 for each additional book) $ _____

■ Additional amount if shipping outside U.S. $ _____

TOTAL ENCLOSED ---------- $ _____

SHIP TO:

Name _____

Address _____

_____

_____

Phone Number: _____

PAYMENT METHOD:

❑ I enclose check/moneyorder for $ _____
   made payable to IMPACT PUBLICATIONS.

❑ Please charge $ _____ to my credit card:

❑ Visa ❑ MasterCard ❑ American Express ❑ Discover

Card # _____

Expiration date: _____/_____

Signature _____

MORE
Travel-Shopping Guides
from Impact
PUBLICATIONS

"You learn more *about a place you are visiting when Impact is pointing the way."*

— **Washington Post**

"An excellent, exhaustive and fascinating *look at shopping."*

— **Travel and Leisure**

Emphasizing the "best of the best" in travel and shopping, the unique Impact Guides take today's discerning travelers into the fascinating worlds of artists, craftspeople, and shopkeepers where they can have a wonderful time discovering quality products and meeting talented, interesting, and friendly people. Each guide is jam-packed with practical travel tips, bargaining strategies, key shopping rules, and recommended shops, hotels, restaurants, sightseeing, and entertainment. The only travel guides that truly promote and support indigenous arts, crafts, and entrepreneurship as well as show how to have a five-star travel-shopping adventure on a less than stellar budget!

*www.*impactpublications*.com*
*www.*ishoparoundtheworld*.com*

MEET talented artisans in India and Egypt

The Treasures and Pleasures of
India

Uncovers India's finest treasures and pleasures in the streets, bazaars, and shopping arcades of nine Indias—Mumbai (Bombay), Delhi, Varanasi, Agra, Jaipur, Jodhpur, Udaipur, Hyderabad, and Chennai (Madras). Reveals 21 shopping rules applicable to most of India. Outlines 12 rules for bargaining. Includes tips on handling touts, packing, shipping, tipping, and baksheesh. Shows the what, where, and how of quality shopping in each city. Details the best hotels, restaurants, sightseeing, and entertainment. 2000. ISBN 1-57023-056-0. $16.95. Tel. 1-800-361-1055.

The Treasures and Pleasures of
Egypt

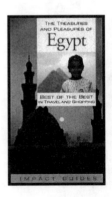

Brings to life Egypt's many exotic bazaars and fine shops, restaurants, hotels, and entertainment venues. Revealing the best travel and shopping in Cairo, Alexandria, Luxor, Aswan, and Sharm el-Sheikh, this unique guidebook includes everything from pre-trip planning to outlining essential shopping rules and identifying the top shops, restaurants, and hotels. From visiting Cairo's grand Khan el-Khalili market to exploring shopping centers, factories, and out-of- the-way shops, travelers discover what to buy, where to shop, and how to bargain for the best deals possible on jewelry, carpets, handicrafts, clothes, textiles, brassware, antiques, ceramics, alabaster, and leather goods. 2001. ISBN 1-57023-149-3. $16.95. Tel. 1-800-361-1055.

DISCOVER the Unique Treasures of
Morocco
and Vietnam

The Treasures and Pleasures of
Morocco

Examines the many travel pleasures and shopping treasures found in one of North Africa's most popular destinations. Covers Casablanca, Rabat, Tangier, Meknes, Fez, Marrakesh, Erfoud, Quarzazate, Tarroudant, Agadir, and Essaouira. Includes shopping strategies, bargaining tips, avoiding problems, selecting quality products, and shipping purchases home with ease. It also identifies the best shops, restaurants, accommodations, sightseeing, and entertainment. Includes a special chapter on Tunisia. August 2001. ISBN 1-57023-163-X. $16.95. Tel. 1-800-361-1055.

The Treasures and Pleasures of
Vietnam

Surprising Vietnam is all about shopping these days! This unique travel-shopping guide examines the many travel pleasures and shopping treasures found in three of Vietnam's major destinations – Hanoi, Danang/Hoi An, and Saigon. Covers everything from Vietnam's top art galleries and markets to tailoring, handicrafts, and pirated goods. Includes shopping strategies and bargaining tips, as well as advice on avoiding problems, selecting quality products, and shipping purchases home with ease. Includes the best restaurants, accommodations, sightseeing, and entertainment. November 2001. ISBN 1-57023-156-7. $16.95. Tel. 1-800-361-1055.